Distant Horizons

As Seen by Williamsburg Poets

Edited by Ron Landa and Edward W. Lull

2013

All rights reserved. No part of this book may be reproduced in any manner, including Internet, without written permission of the authors and editors. No patent liability is assumed with respect to the use of the information contained herein. Although every precaution has been taken in the preparation of this book, the publisher and authors assume no responsibility for errors or omissions. Neither is any liability assumed for damages resulting from the use of the information contained herein.

Copyright © 2013 by Williamsburg Poetry Workshop and James City Poets.

ISBN 978-0-7414-9656-0
Library of Congress Control Number: 2013909839

Printed in the United States of America

Published June 2013

INFINITY PUBLISHING
1094 New DeHaven Street, Suite 100
West Conshohocken, PA 19428-2713
Toll-free (877) BUY BOOK
Local Phone (610) 941-9999
Fax (610) 941-9959
Info@buybooksontheweb.com
www.buybooksontheweb.com

Contents

Preface i

Poems 1

Flora Bolling Adams
No Pedestrians in the Tunnel 3
Early Signs of Spring (An Ottava Rima) 5
The Glove 6
Cutting Roses (After Reading William Carlos Williams) ... 7
A Piece of String (A Villanelle) 8
The Finitude of Youth 9

Angela Anselmo
Portrait 10
Threshold 11
Sixpence 12
Western Sounds 13
Baseball Haiku 14
October Lies About Her Age 15

Norma Beuschel
Celia 16
Pearl 17
Microaviary 18
Arthur Zuar Smith 19
Although It's Tough, You Ought to Plough Through 20
Till Death Do Us Part 21

Ann Marie Boyden
Twelfth-Grade English 22
Valentine 24
Hummingbird 25
Faux Toile 26
Wet Blanket 27
Crossing Memorial Bridge 28

Joan Ellen Casey
Living His Dream 29

Christos de los Andes 33
Oriente 35

Thayer Cory
Epiphany 36
Amagansett 37
Elegy for Suzanne 38
Subway 39
Sisyphus 40
Planting Onions 41

Gillian Dawson
New World 42
Mexicali Roads 43
My Grandmother's Garden 44
Sweet Uses of Adversity 45
A World with Birds 46
Two Gardens 47

Ron Landa
The Old Man and the C 48
Making the Most of It 49
Broken Bough (and Vow) 50
Itterations 51
Past and Future Tents 52
Chesterton Never Did the Mambo 53

Don Loop
Lesson from an "Eight-Year" Old 54
Leaves 55
The Oyster Festival 56
Blue Butterflies 58
Two Crows Walking 59
God-Play 60

Edward W. Lull
My Love 61
The New Dominion 62
Lest We Forget 64
King of Equality 66
Time for Change? (A Ballade) 67
Cristoforo Colombo 68

Marty Mullendore
Autumn Observation ... 70
Covenant with Death ... 71
The Blind Date ... 72
Near Interlaken ... 73
An Investigation into the Soles of Men ... 74
A Perfect Symmetry ... 76

Adele Richards Oberhelman
The Blueridge ... 77
My Unsung Hero ... 78
A Promise in Pink ... 79
Aurora Borealis ... 80
I Spring Eternal ... 81
Celebrating Technology, or What Are We All Smiling About? ... 82

Linda Partee
Just Like Me ... 83
Pomp & Circumstances ... 84
Homemade Preserves ... 85
Just the Tip of the Iceberg (A Sonnet) ... 86
Wavelength ... 87
So Hearts Will Sing (A Triolet) ... 88

Mark Reardon
Sacred Ground ... 89
The Pleasure of the Mountain ... 91
Lake George Morn ... 92
How Do We Begin to Heal? ... 93
Christmas Mittens ... 94
The Color Had All Been Taken Away ... 95

Terry Shepard
Elegy for Ricky ... 96
My Poet Path ... 97
Mid-September ... 98
My Little Town ... 99
Mother Oak ... 100
Groundhog Day ... 101

Edith Piedmont Stoke
Enough Sense to Go Out in the Rain ... 102

Essence 103
Contrails 104
Another Visit 105
The Motherline Is a Circle 106
Hearthcall 107

PETER TRAINOR
Dawn: Nuevo Vallarta, Mexico 108
Maine 110
Womb of Life 111
The Entertainer 112
The Ending 113
9/11/11 114

Contributors 115

Preface

Williamsburg, where the Poetry Society of Virginia was founded in 1923, has in recent years witnessed an upsurge in poetry activity.

Since 2000 the town has played host to an annual poetry festival, a three-day affair with prominent guest speakers and workshops on various aspects of the craft. Monthly poetry readings, attracting people from all over the state, take place at the local library. Coffee houses also serve as venues for regular readings. The Christopher Wren Association, an adult education program of the College of William & Mary, offers poetry-writing classes. Each year the college also sponsors a presentation by an internationally acclaimed writer. They have included former Poets Laureate of the United States Billy Collins and Rita Dove and Nobel Prize winner Seamus Heaney. The current Poet Laureate of Virginia, Sofia Starnes, resides in Williamsburg.

This anthology represents further evidence of the increased activity. It features the poems of seventeen members of two groups: the Williamsburg Poetry Workshop and the James City Poets. Poems range from the traditional to more free-wheeling modern, from lyrical to light verse reminiscent of Ogden Nash, from structured form poetry to free verse. The groups strive to create a friendly environment that encourages development of poetry-writing talents through regular writing, presenting, and critiquing one another's work.

The Williamsburg Poetry Workshop had its beginning in September 2001. Phyllis Haislip and Angela Anselmo, who conceived the idea, hoped a workshop would appeal to both beginners and more advanced writers. Phyllis was in the process of publishing her first children's book; Angela had been writing poetry for ten years and had attended workshops on Long Island.

Only six people attended the first meeting, but the workshop, which met regularly, began to attract a larger, diverse group. Most participants were retirees, some were still working, and a few were in their thirties. An occasional high school or college student took part. By 2009, growth in membership, plus the need to accommodate graduates of the Christopher Wren classes, led to the formation of another workshop: the James City Poets.

We wish to thank Ken Landa of Kenric Graphics for designing the book and Joan Casey, Thayer Cory, Marty Mullendore, and Linda

Partee for their assistance in proofreading and preparing it for publication. Finally, thanks to all our fellow workshop members, including those who chose not to include their poetry, for their perceptive suggestions during working sessions.

Ron Landa and Ed Lull
Williamsburg, Virginia

POEMS

Flora Bolling Adams

No Pedestrians in the Tunnel

We can't go through the tunnel.
No pedestrians in the tunnel!
No traffic through the tunnel!
The sign's in black and white!

Whatever is the problem?
No pedestrians in the tunnel?
No traffic through the tunnel?
The backup is a sight.

Go tell it to the mayor.
Get word out to the mayor;
Go fast, wake up the mayor,
And she will make it right.

What shall I tell Her Highness?
Her Honor or Her Highness?
I cannot speak for shyness.
I fear she'll give me fright.

Five ducks are in the tunnel, Ma'am.
Go tell it to the sheriff. Bam!
She kicked the door and made it slam.
Who the heck do you think I am?

Five ducks are in the tunnel, Sir.
Whatever are they doing there?
Quack-quacking through the tunnel, Sir.
Walking the double line.
Two ducks before two ducks,
Two ducks behind two ducks,
Two ducks between two ducks.
The drake is dragging behind.

My deputy you must go and tell;
(A line like that is hard to sell!)
I fear he won't be feeling well;
Be sure to make it kind.

Five ducks are in the tunnel,
Quack-quacking through the tunnel,
Waddling through the tunnel,
Walking the double line.

Loud and clear I hear your plea.
I can foretell no tragedy.
Rescuing ducks out on a spree
Is simple duck soup for the deputy.
Hurry on back and you will see
Those ducks just needed time that's free.

The ducks are on the pond now. Gee!
And traffic's moving both ways. Whee!
The town is running normally.
They passed the buck on down to me.
Law and order's working, la-de-de.

Early Signs of Spring
(An Ottava Rima)

Dense fog hangs low over the village dreary;
A heart is sad within a troubled breast;
Like superstitious fears, his calls are eerie.
Where is his mate to help him build the nest?
As sun shines through, he hears an answer cheery;
Obediently, she comes at his behest.
He preens and struts; they've many songs to sing;
The air is clear. The robins are here. It's spring!

— Flora Bolling Adams

The Glove

A leather glove is in my drawer,
   No sense of life within its fold.
It speaks to me of loneliness
   And faints away within my hold.
It is as I, and it is mine;
   There is communion here, divine.
Its sense of loss does not abate;
   I tell it I, too, miss my mate.

Cutting Roses
(After Reading
William Carlos Williams)

The pendulum has swung.
It is time to cut the roses.
Old Man Frost will be lurking
in the night like the demon he is.

Please don't cut these roses yet.
They brighten my days out here where they are.
But Old Man Frost—
you know him.
He will nip the very edge
of each petal,
and when the sun comes out,
they will be limp and brown.
Now, as I clip them, put them
in your apron; the thorns are anxious,
worse than the claws of a furious feline.
Do it tomorrow when the stream is clear,
and my head is clear,
the vase is clear,
when everything that matters is clear.
Do it after the fog rolls out
in the morning.
Then perhaps, it will be clear to me
why the roses here by the outhouse,
when cold weather threatens,
are the most beautiful of all.

— Flora Bolling Adams

A Piece of String
(A Villanelle)

A string, a string! It was just a piece of string.
  Being guilty of lying he denied.
The old peasant wouldn't think of such a thing.

An honor to himself he tried to bring.
  'Twas not a purse as his accuser implied.
A string, a string! It was just a piece of string.

Not a purse of value or a golden ring,
  The mayor's smile his scornful words belied.
The old peasant wouldn't think of such a thing.

No honor to himself could keeping bring.
  To be called Old Rascal hurt his pride.
A string, a string! It was just a piece of string.

The purse was found and taken to the king.
  He still was called a thief and vilified.
The old peasant wouldn't think of such a thing.

"My heart is heavy," he cried to the king.
  "No one believes me," he cried and cried.
A string, a string! It was just a piece of string.
His deathbed phrase was, "Just a piece of string."

The Finitude of Youth

A juicy plum is what it was, there
Swinging in the sun,
Dewy star-glaze, heart like pearl,
Strands of sweetened gold were spun.

Yellow jackets in Gold Braid
Flew in to sip—a rune in tune—
In dimpled time the firmness sagged.
Now juicy plum is wrinkled prune.

But it's a sweet old thing.

Flora Bolling Adams

Angela Anselmo

Portrait

I remember the day I bought it.
There was excitement in the gallery
lined with hazy landscapes, modest graphics
and a vague, yet unmistakable likeness
of Marc that I had to have for its artistry
and its promise.

Marc had begged me to accompany him
to the exhibition: "Mother, I want you to meet
her and see her work."
I went, and I too was captivated by the charm
of the lovely young woman
with the smoky gray eyes.

Since then I have looked often at the portrait
hoping for the success of the delightful
young artist and the romance
between her and Marc.

Today Marc called to say
he would be coming home next week.
Alone.

With sadness, I take the portrait,
still in its original frame, from the wall
where it has hung for nearly two years.
I wrap it protectively in one of Marc's
old flannel shirts before
I hide it away.
I wonder if he'll ask about it.

Threshold

Shabby bungalows set at right angles
to the ocean line the run-down streets.

Their sagging porches yield
beneath tired rocking chairs.

Windows, like eyes morose with grime,
show the gloom of desertion.

At the street's end
vagabond sand whirls and drifts,

and just beyond
the bold and ageless ocean

keeps on pounding, thrashing,
never tiring, never weakening,

always demanding change
along its edge.

———— *Angela Anselmo*

Sixpence

Depressed job market
Stubborn unemployment
Increasing debt.
        Today a break at last.
Eli has been hired
by a ski resort
five hundred miles away.
Start next week.
Housing provided.
        "We must elope,"
he persuades Anna.
"No deficit spending
for a fancy wedding."

In a small mountain town
before the justice of the peace,
Anna and Eli exchange vows
and think about what their
families will say
        tomorrow.

With nothing old, nothing new,
nothing borrowed and nothing blue,
the bride wears a sixpence in her shoe.
        The very same coin
her father gave her years ago
when he told her about that old
wedding day tradition.
        The memory brings
her comfort and a warm feeling
that all will go well.

Western Sounds

It speaks a language all its own,
the landscape of the West.
It speaks to me

in lively sounds that
beat like Apache drums
over buttes and mesas,

ring like Hopi pipes
through mesquite and creosote,
ponderosa and pinyon.

Prickly pear and yucca
rattle in my ears like
snakes over rocky ground

and chaparral whispers
on the highest peaks.

Angela Anselmo

Baseball Haiku

Nine men positioned
according to their talent
dare the possible.

Leadoff man a threat
runner teases, pitcher pivots
pick-off makes the out.

Count: three balls two strikes
batter and pitcher duel
shortstop settles it.

The double play
coordinated defense
misguided offense.

Run-of-the-mill stats
end of his rookie season
tonight—a Grand Slam!

The dirty diamond
where stealing is a virtue
thieves become heroes.

Four balls = walk
a leisurely stroll to first
speed not needed here.

To err is human
when an out is the outcome
there is no pardon.

Bottom of the ninth
no score, two out, batter up
BAM, no no-hitter.

Angela Anselmo

October Lies About Her Age

Some days
under sapphire skies
she keeps a frisky pace.
She does a lively dance
as sweet breezes swirl
the golden leaves in her hair.

Some days
she lounges, lazy and light
as a summer day,
offering ripe fruit
and a brilliant moon.

At times she waves
her wicked wand;
changes the soft breeze
to wailing wind,
the leaves to dry scraps.

Grieved by advancing age,
she tries to hide her fading charm
as each day she steals
a little daylight from the sky.

Some call her Indian summer
because she can't be trusted
to behave or tell the truth
about her age.

She calls herself October
meaning *Eight*
in the marching of the year.
No matter how she masquerades,
we know she is really *Ten*.

———————— Angela Anselmo

NORMA BEUSCHEL

Celia

My aunt Celia killed herself
By inhaling gas
Through a rubber hose
In the bathroom
Of a tenement in Brooklyn
In the middle of her life,
In the middle of the night,
In the middle of winter,
In the middle of the Depression.

Eight of us, three generations,
Lived in that cramped, cold-water railroad flat,
In poverty without privacy or dignity,
Stifling in summer, freezing in winter.
It was our confining world.
I, still very young,
Knew that this for me was the bottom rung
Of the ladder I must climb to change my fate.
For Celia it was too late
To escape the cage of her life.

In the twelve years that we lived together,
She gave me the incomparable gift of classical music.
With her meager factory worker's salary,
She would buy recordings
Of operatic arias, of concertos, of symphonies
Played over and over again on her wind-up Victrola.
It was she who took me to stand at the old Met,
To the Brooklyn Academy of Music to hear the glorious voices
Of Lawrence Tibbett and John McCormack.
In the dead of winter, she would go to the piano
In the freezing front room of our flat
And speak to me with nocturnes of Chopin,
With the joyous lilts of Debussy and Johann Strauss.
All my life I have rejoiced in her gift to me.
Her picture hangs beside my bed.
Every day I say, "Thank you."

Pearl

At the snazzier end of my Brooklyn block lived a girl
With the lovely name of Pearl
Eckawee.
She had everything that I wanted
And was everything that I wanted
To be.

In her middy blouse and gym bloomers, she was a flower,
Whereas I looked like a glower-
ing moose. She was everything I was not.
I was brainy, but she was hot.
She was a swan, I was a goose.
She was acute, I obtuse.

Her family could afford Kleenex!
We were so poor that I was ex-
pected to use one dank handkerchief all day.
But she could use a tissue once and throw it away.

The color of envy is a clear, intense green.

Her crowning glory was hard to beat.
In her spacious apartment, she had STEAM HEAT!
Many an icy winter's night
Did I covet her radiators glowing bright.

I often think of Pearl Eckawee.
Has life been as good to her as it has to me?
I could google her, but I prefer to embrace the uncertainty.

Norma Beuschel

Microaviary

I don't fear birds.
Unlike my granddutter,
I lure them with seeds
And peanut butter.

But birds have their place
And I have mine.
One of us
Has crossed the line.

How they got there
Is the answer I crave.
Birds are nesting
Behind my microwave!

Nest in a tree
In the soft spring air.
Not through a labyrinth
To a dark, cramped lair.

At first I thought
I had rats or mice
Or, more alarming,
A poltergeist.

But the chirping and twittering
I have heard
Can come from none other
Than a baby bird.

"How long are you staying?"
I want to shout.
"Does your mother remember
How to lead you out?"

Tonight, when I heat
My *Lean Cuisine*,
Will I be guilty
Of crimes obscene?

"When you finally leave,
You'll take fond farewells with you.
Please also remember
To take your shells with you."

Norma Beuschel

Arthur Zuar Smith

Like his name, Arthur was an ordinary looking man
With a surprise inside.
He was also an incurable stutterer.

His first word would come marching forth proudly, banners flying,
Then lapse into hesitation
Before sinking to a stumbling and gaping halt.
His audience, rapt by his incipient repartee,
Could not refrain from finishing his sentences
Out of a combination of empathy, frustration, and mere impatience.
Arthur, always gracious, would smile broadly
As if those mediocre expressions were exactly
What he had intended to say.

Aware of his affliction, his bosses at RCA had banished him
To an isolate spot where witticisms
Were not a prerequisite—the island of Guam,
To whose populace English was a second language
Which they spoke only in broad strokes,
And who could not tell a *bon mot* from a banana.

Arthur lived in the Quonset hut next to ours.
We shared the shimmering brilliance of every sunrise
And the heart-gladdening vista of the golden coastline.

Arthur's wife, a large, loud lady with a lazy eye,
Was chief sentence finisher
And tried to anticipate each faltering utterance.
As an orator, Arthur was doomed.

Decades later, widowed and in a nursing home,
Through a medical coincidence Arthur regained his dormant ability.
A side effect of his prescribed drug returned to him
The gift of clear, unfettered speech.
And speak he did!
Fluently, brilliantly, volubly, stentorianly.

But there was nobody left to listen.

— Norma Beuschel

Although It's Tough, You Ought to Plough Through

Why is English not phonetic?
Grammatically it is pathetic,
Its pronunciation abysmal,
Its spelling cataclysmal.
(What's your theory, dearie?)
You are driving on a road,
But add a "b" and the road is broad.
As you rode, did you become awed?
If I enjoy a book today, I read;
But yesterday, perhaps in bed, I read.
Or so I said!
Can you hear the bear with bare hair?
It's not here—it's over there, ready to scare.
See those does? A doe does eat dough, no?
(Does the laughing calf know?)
Is there any sort of plasma
That can cure the miasma of my asthma?
Since the plural of house is houses,
May I assume that a mouse duo is mouses?
(Why not, honestly, honey?)
What! The plural of mouse is mice?
So, more than one spouse is spice?
As for lie and lay, fuhgeddaboutit.
Ask any American if you subtly doubt it.
The weight of the bait is great and first-rate,
But the height of the kite is not right.
(Good luck with that, ESL students.)
Goose becomes geese,
But a mongoose duet is mongooses.
Sarah Palin, is it meese or mooses that you shooteth?
Can you bear it that our spelling so loose is?
I understand faked and raked and baked,
But of which verb is the past tense naked?
Why is the milk so mild?
Is that giraffe a girl?
You knew a pseudo gnu at the zoo? Cute!
After rowing and hoeing, Rhoda put on a bow
And took a bow under the bough. Wow!
I bet that causes quite a row.
A picture is hung, but an adulteress is hanged.
Or did they stone her and her family disown her?
Consider, please, colonel and kernel,
Kansas and Arkansas.

Norma Beuschel

Till Death Do Us Part

It was a marriage like many others,
Unhappy but enduring,
Catholic, many children.
Mutual hatred.
He bad-tempered, domineering, a mean drunk.
She submissive, resentful, resigned.

He died first, young, heavy drinker.
Cremated, ashes in an urn on a closet shelf.
Disguising her elation, she shed the required tears.
Cleared the house of his belongings.
Putting him out of her mind,
She enjoyed decades of peace.
Simple joys . . . church, friends, family.
Children all grown, she was completely free.

At her death, still very religious, she requested burial.
Her children complied.
At the last moment, on a whim,
They put the urn containing his ashes
In a corner of the coffin
Near her head.
And closed the lid.
Buried. Together.

— Norma Beuschel

Ann Marie Boyden

Whan that aprill with his shoures soote
The droghte of march hath perced to the roote,
And bathed every veyne in swich licour
Of which vertu engendred is the flour. . . .

                Geoffrey Chaucer

Twelfth-Grade English

Pansy Powell's first-period English:
all the cool kids were there. Football
and basketball jocks, track stars,

cheerleaders, prom and drama queens.
Surprisingly, most of them studied.
There were a few of the rest: squares,

lunchers, cornballs. Members of the
Marching Band and ROTCies, both in
uniform. A greaser was in uniform, too:

Elvis hair, tight levis, and leather jacket.
Some of the rest did not study at all.
By tall windows in western winter light

sat two who thought they were writers,
listening carefully as Miss Powell stood
at the blackboard where a weird poem

was written in white chalk and Middle
English. "*The Canterbury Tales* is one
of the greatest poems ever written,"

she said. The assignment: memorize
these eighteen lines of the prologue—
be prepared to recite it—with correct

pronunciation. Miss Powell demonstrated.
More than half actually memorized it;
the first person called on to recite had not.

The next two, both ROTCies, had.
A clarinet player, a square, the greaser,
and the writers all struggled through it.

A jock recited fast enough to set a record.
A drama queen ACTED! I was in that class
and still remember—the first four lines anyway.

Valentine

Her bright blue phone vibrates.
The girl with the auburn hair
listening to the man droning on
about the War of 1812 slips
the phone from her pocket
and glances down at the screen
without tipping her head.

"b my v tine
c u   luv J"

The girl with the auburn hair
and the fancy phone
feels her heart beating and smiles.
There is no lace doily or
hearts or red roses,
no chocolate or diamonds,
but as far as the girl
with the auburn hair is concerned
J cared enough to send the very best.

Hummingbird

I held a hummingbird in my hand.
There was nothing there but life.
A perfect creature bound by silk
rescued from a spider's lair.
I pulled the sticky tangles from his
long beak, little feet, tiny silver
tail, and at last his wings.
Suddenly he flew.

Later, I saw him at the feeder.
There was a silver thread
hanging from his back.
He hovered in midair
with bright blue wings a blur,
he looked me in the eye,
and flew away.

—*Ann Marie Boyden*

Faux Toile

The woman strides purposely toward
a corner table, her faux toile dress in
black and white clinging tightly
to her muffin top and sagging breasts.
Spaghetti straps press into her soft shoulders.
It's all-you-can-eat crab-legs night.

A younger woman, with a sweater draped
over her shoulders because of the air-
conditioning, sucks on a leg as the pile
of crustacean carcasses in the middle
of the table grows. Outside, the temperature
is ninety-nine degrees.

Are the two friends, sisters, lovers?
Or is the younger one the faux toile
woman's daughter? Hair the same bleached
blond, noses alike, they stand up to leave.
The younger one pulls off the sweater
and throws it over her arm.

She wears a too-tight tank top that reveals nipples
and navel. Her skirt is appropriate to a production
of *Swan Lake*. Seriously, it's a tutu!
Now it's clear. Mother and daughter,
with the same nose and the same
taste in fashion.

Wet Blanket

In a box somewhere there is a photograph of you,
or perhaps the picture is only in my mind.
You are sitting on the ugly, pink Danish-modern
sofa my sorority sister gave me for that perfectly
awful apartment on F Street. You are sitting
there with a beer in your hand and a slice of
cold pizza on your bare knee. We've been
playing in the pool, and your damp hair is pasted
to your head like a little boy's. Your wet trunks
are creating a surprise for the next person
to sit there.

I know now that this is the last time we'll be
together like this, with friends and beer and pizza,
because although it was hard then—
it was right to tell you to get lost.
We were wasting our time—because
you thought I was wasting my time,
writing poetry.

Ann Marie Boyden

Crossing Memorial Bridge

It's the long way to the District—Lee Highway,
Spout Run—rag top folded in the summer
haze—forested gully, mist clings to trees,
there are surely ghosts here.
Parkway, Roosevelt Island, Arlington
roundabout. In heavy summer
the eternal flame flickers above
Lincoln's Doric temple. In every season,
this drive is a pilgrimage. A pilgrimage
to November 25, 1963—limbers and caisson,
flag-draped casket, color guard, riderless horse.
Huge gilded stallions bear witness to grief.
Long black limousines fill the bridge—
mourners, schemers, dictators, presidents,
politicians, a widow and two brothers.
The world is changed forever.
Still, every morning, after all these years,
the flame burns on the hill.

Joan Ellen Casey

Living His Dream

"A good provider," Mother said of Dad.
So little else I knew of him, except
his love for boats and fishing—anytime.
He picked first mates for friends and worked in dock,
outfitting ships to carry loads by sea.
I went to him one day to say I'd leave,
to ski the snows in South America.
"If leave you must, then go by ship," he said.

> The time had come before I knew.
> With gangplank, anchor gone from view,
> my boat just gently slid from shore,
> like leaving land and nothing more.
>
> With damp adhering to my skin
> and feeling waves awash within,
> I watched the tugboats dragging load,
> not thinking channel was a road.
>
> My misted eyes looked back to see
> no albatross had shadowed me;
> though hungry seagulls followed fast
> till open water grew more vast.

The sight of Lady Liberty's raised torch
reminded me of those who'd come ashore
in search of freedom, fortune, promised dreams,
and leaving family to memory.
Excited by the trip ahead, I knew
my choice to leave might bring both grief and loss;
but thoughts soon turned to fathomed depths I saw—
the sea's vast stretch had stunned my breath and soul.

> My room was big enough for two,
> but passengers were all too few.
> Beyond porthole was a pool,
> though all too small and pitiful.

Each meal I took at Captain's table,
with Dutchman not of flying fable,
who told us tales at ev'ry meal
and even let me take ship's wheel.

Besides a tour of engine's room
and lifeboats' place in case of doom,
there wasn't anything to do
and little contact with the crew.

I sat on deck and drank the captain's beer,
and talked to George about the books he'd read.
Frau Ruth and Hans retold their grandkids' pranks;
and quiet Paulo smiled at all I said.
The purser came to be a friend and spent
off-duty time just playing cards with me.
I won a night's free stay in Trinidad
but thought of Dad and times I played with him.

The world was blue both day and night.
Just hue was changed by dark or light.
The water, restless, seldom slept;
horizon there but never met.

The mystic spell of cloud and sea
had let the beat of time run free.
Monotony, monotony—
the only voice of revelry.

Each day of facing into wind
I grew increasingly thin-skinned.
Protective walls for shutting out
were falling, crumbling, strewn about.

I never knew what fight I had gone through
relieving crush of bodies on my skin,
or holding back the sounds invading thought—
sensations' seas that flood a crowded mind.
For once, alone with little else, I was
just drifting midst some feelings new to me.
Afloat, alive, awake to whole of peace,
in comfort being nothing else at all.

Arriving at first port of trip,
excitedly I left the ship
and walked the streets of Trinidad
soon feeling sorry, sick, and sad.

The ground just heaved beneath my feet.
Too nauseous to even eat,
with dizziness that made me faint,
I was not once without complaint.

The room I had so wanted won,
had turned out not to be much fun.
Though I remained so well at sea,
the land now wrought a scourge on me.

Once back on board, the well-accustomed few
assured me I would claim my balance soon.
But meanwhile, water pounded freighter's hull.
Where northern met the southern easterlies,
mid slip of sea near coast of Africa,
the wind with fury drove the crew below.
Though shaken, frightened, shocked, yet thrilled—I stayed
on deck to witness nature's play of wrath.

The sea now sick and heaving rage
with nothing left that could assuage
what thrashing, roiling waves so wrought
against our ship that bowed and fought.

The clamor went on hour by hour,
each time attempting to devour
not only me but what I held—
my wrap, the ropes, and all unquelled.

While wet and winded I stood fast,
determined just to storm outlast,
and found a strength I never knew
with humbleness of spirit, too.

The rush of wind so strong upon my face
had brought to mind the Easter morn at dawn
when I had skied alone through storm downhill.
Complete in feeling one with world and sky

—————————————————————————— *Joan Ellen Casey*

had opened mind's invite to live a thought.
Once choice was made, I was compelled to go—
not thinking I would find along the way
much more than I could even think to dream.

> I watched the day awaken night
> with gentle tones of pastel light.
> The sea was soothed to quiet sleep
> alit with dreams of peace to keep.
>
> As light intensified and grew,
> a path of shimmer made debut,
> with bubbles dancing on the surf
> as newborn birds of nature's scurf.
>
> We headed south along the shore,
> but days of sailing were no more.
> The tanks and weapons in our hold
> had made our destination bold.

A military coup in Argentine
brought end to voyage south of Rio's port.
I went by bus with baggage, skis, and poles,
five days through rain and mud and rice-filled fields.
Sometimes I pushed the bus, sometimes I rode.
At journey's end, I took the longest bath,
then made my way to port to see the ships,
refinding solace watching sea and tide.

> Through months of travel that ensued,
> I missed the sea and quietude
> and often went to see the shore
> to find the peace I sought once more.

At once compelled to leave, but then return,
I flew back home at Christmas time—the last
there was for Dad. I showed my slides and told
my tales of mountains, jungles, ports of call.
I never asked if I had lived a dream
he dreamt; yet wished he wished this trip for me—
to see what world there is and where I fit:
to leave to find my way back home again.

Christos de los Andes

*Sooner shall these mountain crags crumble to dust
than Chile and Argentina shall break this peace
which at the feet of Christ the Redeemer
they have sworn to maintain.*

> Inscription on the Statue of Christ the Redeemer
> that stands in the La Cumbre Pass at 12,572 feet
> above sea level on the border between Argentina
> and Chile, Mt. Aconcagua in view.

It had been a season of skiing sunrise into sunset
until days grew warmer
and shadows longer.

With poles on tractor, my place on tow line,
I began the climb to La Cumbre
thousands of feet high and miles away.

The ride was rough, the haul too short.
What followed was on foot,
watching each slide I took.

Skiers ahead, skiers behind, I kept up as I could,
finding a gait
to haul my weight.

Ascent grew slower as air sank lower.
Nature's clock in the sky
said day was nigh gone by.

The pass had to be crossed before dark would dawn.
The last hurdle was hardest of all
with skis to mountain to brace a fall.

Each move up made legs feel broken and burnt.
Each breath went still
short of lungs' fill.

I pushed one foot to grab air in, one to throw it out,
till rhythm felt more
than the pain I bore.

—*Joan Ellen Casey*

By sound of the snow, I knew we arrived.
All stood in silent awe
of the statue they saw.

Christ, arms outstretched to embrace, loomed at top of rise,
and beyond in empty sky
Aconcagua sat on high.

I thought then of all who had come here before
to fight, to conquer, to build, to praise,
to see a statue that once went to rust
and mountain crags spared crumbling to dust.

Oriente

(Thick Ecuadorian jungle
sparsely populated by civilized tribes
of Quechua and uncivilized
headhunters called Jivaro.)

Green mixed with mud.

Green evaporating into mist
from shallow pools of heat.

Green, loud with insects
tantalizing predators.

Green scratching my eyes,
running from my bowels,
growing on my clothes,
lining my eyelids,
mixing into my rice and beans,
peopling my dreams.

Green walls of jail or refuge.
Green riding the river of endless shore,
searching, ferreting, fearing
all that is not green.

———— Joan Ellen Casey

Thayer Cory

Epiphany

It was two goats,
statue still
behind the fence, their
eyes gray and glassy as marbles

It was the tufts of grass
they stood on,
the clumsy sheep behind them
and the clods of earth
all dark and damp

It was the way, as we
drew near, they inched
stupidly towards Tom
and the way
he scratched their noses

That sent the shards of the
kaleidoscope tumbling,
turning everything
suddenly precious

It was then I knew
that somewhere deep inside
goats sing praises,
sheep rejoice,
grass adores its loveliness
and dirt is lit from within

Amagansett

> *Have you a place where,*
> *when the world ends,*
> *you want to be?*
>
> William Stafford

Here, of course, where the sea
breathes in and out,
a steady pulse of always

where sand-stunted pines
and snarled underbrush
link arms around the house.

Here between the scalloped hem
of the tide line and
the smooth rim of the world

where waves unfurl their ruin,
their primal children,
their whispers: *Listen. Now.*

I will be here where water's colors
rinse the dune and even clouds
have useful things to say

where the dog chases
sandpipers up the beach
and the buoyant moon swims into the night.

Here we gather around the uncomfortable
table, eat bluefish and peaches,
pour old stories from cup to broken cup.

It's here the light of dusk bends over me,
reveals a voice within my voice,
a shadow deeper than my own.

Here a long-ago prayer
from summer's church choir
chants *world without end. Amen. Amen.*

Elegy for Suzanne

> *The best teachers teach more*
> *than they know. By their deaths*
> *they teach most. They lead us beyond*
> *what we know, and what they knew.*
>
> *Wendell Berry*

The peonies, their pale, pink fists still taut,
will burst and flare again though you are gone,
then bend to time's worn hand just as they ought—
the Mystery of bloom and death is one.
You loved your life, but fought with death, enraged
by early loss, an orphaned child's plight.
With fierce and pointed will, you turned and faced
the equal measures brought by Dark and Light.
When cancer came—your heart, encased in grief
for all the joys you'd lose, was filled with fear.
We prayed for Grace—acceptance of the thief
who robs us . . . and brings peonies each year.
The Mystery runs deep in lessons taught—
to wake, to bloom, to die just as we ought.

Subway

Inside the L train at 7:45 am   the faithful
burrow into their   skins   stop ears with
musical buttons   gaze into the middle
distance   or read

Doors gasp open   wide mouths   spit out some
suck in others   close with a sigh   Bullet
hurtles down dusky tunnel   screaming
startingstopping   syncopated wheels   rock
passengers   who appear unmoved

Hands close on poles   or overhead handles
knees and thighs   escape touch   by fractions
of inches   In intimate indifference   with
measured politeness   New York pilgrims
head to   secret   destinations

The schizophrenic   and his dusty dog
careen   through the car   but only the woman
in red tights   and black jacket   is roused
puts change in   his bag

The white gentleman   in natty suit   helps
the grizzled   black man   decipher the map
tells him   where to change trains
The student and his cello hog two   seats

The angelic hipster   with nose ring
and hole in his   ear   the size of a nickel
rises from his reverie   unfolds from his seat
nods his wired head   to the old woman
who shuffles over   takes   his place

Every day   the faithful enter   the silver cocoon
huddle   with strangers   cradle
their stories calculate their space   closeness
distance   awake   asleep   they trust
they   will be   delivered

Sisyphus

One must imagine Sisyphus happy.

Albert Camus

Always the fear—
Happiness will be snatched away.

The gods will peer down and deem a life
too choked with joy, too full of passion.

We will be condemned like Sisyphus,
our burdens forever before us—

The price we must pay
for a life moving forward.

The terrible voices of childhood
rain down like gods, forcing us

to repeat, repeat
to put our whole effort

into pushing the rocks of our dreams
up the mountains in our hearts.

One must imagine Sisyphus happy.
Begin again. And again.

In dogged labor are we tamed,
brought back in consciousness to

what we must learn: Joy is what we bring,
not what we find.

Planting Onions

She is no farmer
but she bends her head
to the earth and knows

its emptiness,
its longing. She has
come to the farm

to plant onions, small
tasseled pearls to be sown
in small wounds

red, white and yellow—
bulbs made snug
in the hopeful soil.

She muses on the row
that's been given her,
measures the four inches

between plantings.
An old anxiety
about doing it perfectly

argues with the knowledge
that the earth is forgiving.
She doubts her place in this world

and lacks the peace of simple things.
But for now her mind is bent
to the darkness before her,

to the dirt that feeds the onions,
that coaxes them dumbly
to take root, to grow.

Gillian Dawson

New World

The order came from high authority,
It traveled down the bureaucratic chain
Until it reached the one who would announce
The opening of the Gate behind the Wall.

They first received the news with disbelief,
Took fearful steps into that no-man's land,
A place of death and danger yesterday,
A few more cautious steps, yet no shots came.

Then throwing caution to the winds, they rushed
Towards that concrete monster, hearts aflame.
They scaled its heights with ease, spurred on by hope
That from its top they'd see a better world.

And on the other side they heard the news,
Flocked to the Wall to see if it were true,
Families separated many years,
Reunited, sang, embraced, shed tears.

Yet still amid their joy they paused to look
At sad memorials to those who died,
Shot while escaping, one of them nine days ago,
Poor soul, he should have waited till this day.

This day that changed our world, that gave us hope,
That saw a wall come down, not one go up.
What will we do with this new world we claimed,
The day the Wall collapsed 'neath Freedom's weight?

Mexicali Roads

There are no atheists in a foxhole, they say.
When the shells burst too close, you curl up and you pray.
My friend and I know, you can take it from us,
There are no atheists on a Mexican bus!

Up mountains we drove on switchback-like roads,
Guardrails too expensive for here, I supposed.
When I looked far below us, my heart filled with fear;
A bus just like ours lay rusting down there!

Lips moving in prayer, their rosaries out,
Those Mexican folks knew what this was about;
Pray for driver and engine, brakes, steering and gears,
"Lord, get us there safely; please answer our prayers."

"We made it," we cried. "*Que milagro;* we're here
gracias a Dios and the power of prayer."
But during this day don't forget how to pray;
This evening we have to go back the same way!

— *Gillian Dawson*

My Grandmother's Garden

Furry, pink and yellow,
the peaches hang ripe and ready to fall
from branches that spread across
red brick walls
warmed by a gentle sun
under the pale blue sky
of an English autumn.
Currant bushes,
their crimson, white and black fruit
gleaming, ready for picking,
stand row upon row,
firm in the deep brown earth.
Purple plums and rosy apples
hide in green foliage,
some overripe, fallen to the ground,
devoured by ants,
sipped by buzzing bees,
their sweet aroma spreading through the air.

This childhood memory
of my grandmother's abundant garden
still invades my senses,
catches me unawares.
I am again in that garden,
hands stained with berry juice,
teeth sunk into the soft flesh of plums,
and I am content, as then.

Sweet Uses of Adversity

There are so many words that describe Adversity:
Unhappiness, misfortune, bad luck and misery,
Calamity, affliction, disaster and distress,
We shun the road that leads to Her and search for happiness.

While there are some who choose to make their life a living hell,
Perceiving some gain so obscure its worth is hard to tell,
The rest of us may find ourselves, through no fault of our own,
Unwilling victims in the clutch of that old grinning crone.

So why does Shakespeare, matchless bard, proclaim in one great play
How sweet can be the uses of that hag Adversity?
Methinks he means Her overcome, the victory surely ours,
When we cast off Her grizzly gown and once more smell the flowers.

Our journey through Adversity gives us the strength to know
That if again we meet with Her we're stronger than our foe,
Gives us compassion, empathy with one another's plight,
The tools and strategies we need to conquer Her dark night.

— Gillian Dawson

A World with Birds

Birds are ancient.
Millions of years before man,
they were here on earth,
when Pterodactyl,
the largest flying animal
ever to exist on our planet,
soared on its cumbersome way
above the land.

Birds are mythical.
The Phoenix, consumed by fire,
rises from the very ashes it created,
signifying rebirth.

Birds are symbolic:
the eagle for freedom,
the dove for peace.

Birds are amazing.
Consider the hummingbird,
the smallest of birds,
beating its wings
three hundred times a second,
like a helicopter
hovers and flies backwards.
How do birds migrate
thousands of miles
over mountains and deserts,
through storms and hurricanes,
and touch down
just where they ought to be?

Birds are messengers.
The red-breasted robin,
the bright-colored warblers
chirping in the treetops,
tell us that Spring is here.

Imagine a world without birds!

Two Gardens

One a garden of delight,
Abundance and perfection,
Eden, garden of creation,
Home of first man and woman.
Yet in its midst the fatal tree,
Forbidden fruit low-hanging,
Tempting, irresistible.
One bite of its crisp flesh
And they would be as God,
The serpent said.
So they ate and fell from grace,
Their lot toil and suffering,
Their end but dust.

Yet through millennia
Of legend and history,
Travel to another garden,
Rock-filled, barren, windswept,
A garden of agony and betrayal,
Gethsemane its name,
Where in acceptance and obedience
Another pledged to give His life
To suffering and death,
Redeeming that first sin
Of man and woman
For all generations.
Creation, Damnation, Salvation:
Two gardens.

Gillian Dawson

Ron Landa

The Old Man and the C

Since childhood it's been my favorite soup,
    and I still love this pretend pond
where I can fish in the kitchen all day
    with a spoon that's more like a magic wand.

There's no limit to what can be reeled in.
    "No Lettering" signs have all been taken down.
From each day's catch, I make anything I want—
    adjectives, verbs, and the occasional noun.

Many letters are lacking in taste,
    on the tongue even a little suspicious.
But last week I snared a big, smiling O
    and knew right off it would be delicious.

When I took a bite from its rounded side,
    the shape became something new.
Now a C, it assumed a crimson color,
    not at all like its old baby blue.

In this glorious red-letter day for me,
    it went from cheery O to shining C!

Making the Most of It

From the Vantage Point, a glass-enclosed
   restaurant atop the hotel, you sometimes can see
the Shrine of the Immaculate Conception
   six miles away across the Potomac.
Not today. A blizzard disgorged
   record-setting snow, a whiteout that left
   nothing visible except swirling flakes.

Inside, not much was happening.
A dozen customers sat alone and silent
at their tables, businessmen over forty,
   several quite a bit—road warriors
accustomed to life on the go—their mood
   darkened by the certainty
of being marooned for a day or two.
A woman with long brown hair
and black turtleneck accentuating her fair
   skin sat in their midst. She looked thirtyish,
but was probably older. The only
   talk was between waiter and customer,
   almost whispered.

Seated close to the woman, a balding man
   with glasses, glancing up repeatedly
from his food to catch her eye, decided
   to break the silence. "Where are you from?"
he asked, loud enough for everyone to hear.
   "Gary," she replied. "Gary, Indiana."
"That's funny," he said quickly, "I used to live
   there." The easy opening encouraged him
   to ask, "May I join you?"

From where I sat, I could see his widening,
   satisfied smile, as she hesitated,
   then said, "Yes."

Broken Bough
(and Vow)

After
we added
several new
ones each year,
ornaments covered
the tree so completely
that it was hard to see the
sagging branches. Hearing a limb
snap, I suddenly remembered the old
English professor who made us promise
to "slay" adjectives. We had done just the opposite.
Believing more was better, we engaged in wanton acquisition
of unneeded
baubles.

Itterations

After all the casual hints and romantic moments
    Jim had carelessly frittered,
Ann doubted he would ever propose
    and was stunned to get gorgeously glittered.
She dreamt of herself as mother of nine, the perfect litter,
    whose slippered feet would go patter-pitter.
But, awakened, she felt a jitter.
    How would they pay for a sitter?

    So she reconsittered.

Jim was a good guy; he wasn't morose or bitter.
    But she could always find someone fitter.
You see, he had trouble making up his mind
    when it involved choices of a similar kind.
To wit: he was completely unsure whether
    the word should be "tweet" or "twitter."

    But so was she.

Decisions! Decisions! They were in such a bind.
    In the end, each remained a single critter.

Past and Future Tents

A wise old Arab shared this sound advice:
    "Don't let a camel get his nose in the tent."
The words could apply to people as well;
    I think that's what the saying must have meant.

Light canvas shelters have such wide appeal;
    they can be moved around quite easily.
But they smell and leak and flood when it rains;
    that's why inside them you'll never find me.

I skipped the Scouts and their camping out;
    to sleep on cold ground made little sense.
And pup tents with no room to breathe
    were unfit for short-term residence.

We loved the parade when the circus arrived;
    the animals we greeted with a hearty yell.
But the Big Top made me deathly afraid;
    I always worried, "What if the trapezists fell?"

Huge wedding parties in lowly Moose Halls,
    where guests could dance to the most recent craze,
were much more fun than posh, tented affairs
    with gouda, Pinot Noir, and canapés.

I once stood in the heat and watched from afar
    while a preacher thrilled a jam-packed tent.
If he saved any souls I could not tell,
    but their wallets suffered a blessed dent.

Our politics depend on the two-tent system
    with rallies, coalitions, and esprit.
But the Parties offer such a sorry choice—
    either a donkey or an elephant be.

So I'll shun any structure the Parties set up;
    they're havens for non-thinkers to hide.
If anyone asks, "Which side are you on?"
    I'll say, "But, of course, the outside."

Chesterton Never Did the Mambo

Though no one considers us fancy hoofers,
we relish the senior center's Saturday night
dance. Waltzes, fox trots,
and most Latin rhythms present
    no-prob-lem.

The mambo is something else. Three
staccato steps, set off by slight pauses,
it requires quick, decisive leads
that overwhelm my ability to
    think-a-head.

We've tried it on the side where
few eyes might notice our clumsiness, but
couldn't get into sync with the music
or one another. Embarrassment was
    hard-to-hide.

Everyone's vulnerable to fears that fuel bad dreams:
stumbling on stage, forgetting lines, singing off-key—
in short, making a bad impression.
And it's no fun looking foolish on
    the-dance-floor.

What better reason, I say, for not trying at all.
Years ago G. K. Chesterton remarked,
"If a thing is worth doing, it's worth doing badly,"
but he didn't know about
    the-mam-bo.

Now, whenever they play "Mambo Italiano"
or "Papa Loves Mambo," we park ourselves
near the punch bowl and munch crackers,
doing what's far more enjoyable—
    the-no-step.

Don Loop

Lesson from an "Eight-Year" Old

My grandson and I were driving—
rather, I was. He was jiving,
oscillating hands and body
to some remembered rock-ody,

'til suddenly he wrenched his head
around, looked at me and said,
"Granddaddy, are you gonna get married?"
Surprised at the way I was queried,

all I could reply was, "Well now . . . ."
He then said, "O.K., I'll tell you how!"
With hand and finger pointed up,
began the lesson from this pup.

"First you find a girl that's pretty.
Then you tell her that she's pretty.
Then you take her some flowers."
"And sing to her of April showers?"

"Next you tell her that you love her."
"Wait just a minute, hold on sir!
You're moving way too fast for me.
Do you have a girlfriend?" "Just three."

"Anyway," holding up his left arm,
"you give her a bracelet with a charm,
like this one. Haven't you seen
one in a bubblegum machine?"

Attention spent by explanation,
he swiveled back to oscillation,
keeping time to an unheard din,
doing "henpecks" with his chin.

Now Hudson's very prescient
to see me as is, life near spent,
no wife, just memories to glean
for want of a bubblegum machine.

Leaves

Time, that thief, has robbed again.
The children all have fledged and gone,
No more to watch them raking leaves,
Or laughing, romping on the lawn.

Fall of the year is coming,
And the fall of my life is here.
Leaves of the trees are turning.
My grand finale draws near.

The leaves of my life are many,
They are colored variously,
Some of them a deep crimson,
Others no color you see.

But the ones which are brightest,
To remember as I grow old,
Are memories gleaned of my children.
Ah! These are the leaves of gold!

Don Loop

The Oyster Festival

An oyster yawned upon a rock,
The Rappahannock flowing by.
"I'm bored," it thought, but couldn't say,
Its primal throat could only sigh.

Its cousin oyster sitting near,
By method telepathic,
Heard the plaintive melody
And waxed sympathetic.

"Go to the Oyster Festival,"
The wise one tely'd back.
"It's in honor of our own kind.
Just ignore that old crab shack!"

"I'll have some fun," it thought, "at that!
For oysters have been specially billed!"
By hoist, by boat, by truck it went,
Then in a bushel box was chilled.

Beneath the tent a stand-up bar,
A hungry salivating crowd.
Just being at the festival
Made the little oyster proud!

So its heart, such as it was,
Felt buoyed up and full
To be among the revelers,
When its life had been so dull.

By nine o'clock the gourmets came
With oysters to be fed.
Just then within its nascent brain
The oyster felt a splash of red.

A sudden motion upward,
It tried, but couldn't yell,
"This isn't what I . . . ."
And down the glutton's throat it fell!

"Go to the Oyster Festival,"
The wise one had suggested.
"Of food there is variety."
Indeed! Our oyster was ingested!

More oysters grow upon the rock,
While we like carpenters cloister
To doff our hats in solemn thanks
And sorrow for the oyster.

———— *Don Loop*

Blue Butterflies

There at the muddy cattle pond,
Inside the cattle gate beyond
The lane I walked from school to home,
Up rose a cloud of butterflies
Bluer than icy, pale blue skies.

As any six-year old would do,
I stood and stared while round they flew
Above indented milk-cow tracks.
Lost in a boyhood reverie,
I felt that they were one with me.

But then my stomach beckoned me,
And woke me from that mesmerie
As hunger drove away the dream.
So up the graveled hill I went,
On food by now my thought intent.

Mom from inside said, "Wipe your feet,
Come in and get a cookie treat!"
Then she said, "Y'all go outside."
I took my sister who was four
And headed out the kitchen door.

Outside a cow had just lay down
On pasture grass. We sneaked around
To her backside. She turned and looked.
We climbed right up on her slick hide
And did a bovine belly slide.

Rump first she stood and off she went.
We laughed out loud in merriment.
Perhaps we'd chase some hens—that's fun.
Or go and make some piglets squeal
By taking them from mama's meal.

We have no toys like that today.
Nor joys to while the time away.
Has "Truth broke in," as Frost once said,
And left us only dreams of youth,
Within a world that's grown uncouth?

Two Crows Walking

Two crows I saw a-walking down
A railroad rail outside of town,
In suits with tails the blackest black
With purpose down that railroad track.

It would be speculation to
Presume to know what they would do,
Or where the two had planned to go
While putting on an avian show.

Performers in an Ink Spots band,
With one a saxophone in hand?
Perhaps just dandies on the town
To which the pair were strolling down.

Of course I am curious why
These wing-ed ones declined to fly,
Unless to them 'twas sport to see
This nosey, puzzling wing-less me.

It is a human being's trait
To wonder and to speculate.
The answer to those tandem birds
Is past our ken or poet's words!

God-Play

On Mt. Helicon in Greece,
Where Apollo and the Muses
Played beside the sacred spring
Hippocrene, they devised
A game with mischief in their mind
That would forever pique mankind.

Then, like seeds of myriad
Ripe and bursted milkweed pods,
Came down the germ of poignant wit
Broad-scattered by the avid gods.
To speak in verse, mankind was taught
A way of organizing thought

And words superior to prose.
Their sentences arranged in ranks
Bore Eros's enchanted lance
Enhancing earth's distraught lovers,
As some love-stricken youth did win
His miss by his verse-dripping pen.

The sanctuaries of the world
Resound with poems made hymnody.
The love of Venus for Adonis,
Though did sadly come to naught,
Her poems had not entranced him
To save him from the pig that lanced him.

Ares saw sacrificed-to-war
Warriors lifted up by anthem,
The battle hymn that emboldens,
With blood-sanctifying trenches.
The gods were indiscriminate
When engendering love or hate.

Gods, too, warred among themselves,
As ancient poets have told us.
Thank God those mythic gods of Greece
Hold forth no longer on the mount,
Have faded to antiquity.
But bless them who gave us poetry!

Edward W. Lull

My Love

I've never met one like her, that I know;
her pure commitment to me makes me strong.
My work keeps me quite busy now, although
she whiles away the hours all day long.

Her looks are not exceptional, I guess,
but beauty wasn't what I sought from her.
Companionship, without a lot of stress
and not excessive talking, I prefer.

She's getting rather paunchy, I admit,
but she finds exercise no longer fun.
At dinner time I hardly get to sit
before I note that she's completely done.

> But looks and manners never will prevail;
> I know I'm loved—the way she wags her tail.

The New Dominion

Both nobly born and common man
from England crossed the sea,
and thus the Commonwealth began
with those who would be free
to spread themselves across the land
and settle where they could.
With hardships greater than they planned,
they still found freedom good.

    The Old Dominion lives anew,
    proud gem of USA.

From sturdy stock their leaders grew
with independent thought.
Protecting liberty, they knew,
could not be simply bought.
The price was high, but fully paid,
as brave men's blood was shed.
A nation then was loosely made;
Virginia's statesmen led.

    The Old Dominion lives anew,
    proud gem of USA.

The Commonwealth's diversity—
its greatest attribute,
with fishing from the bay and sea
and orchards filled with fruit.
The Shenandoah farms provide
fine food for rich and poor.
The massive rivers, long and wide,
link Blue Ridge to the shore.

    The Old Dominion lives anew,
    proud gem of USA.

The tempo of commercial North
contrasts with Southern pace.
The Eastern watermen go forth,
a wind-tossed sea to face.
A home for all who would be true
to those who paved the way,
the Old Dominion lives anew,
proud gem of USA.

Edward W. Lull

Lest We Forget

Dogwood trees and buttercups
appear to almost shine.
Springtime's glory never fails
North Creek at Brandywine.
Forebears gave their lives.

Tassels tossed by gentle winds,
corn stalks tall and sleek;
dusty road and stony bridge
at Antietam Creek.
Soldiers fell en masse.

Morning mist engulfs the trees,
birds singing as they should;
later sunbeams burn their paths
into Belleau Wood.
Many never left.

Trees with tangled, twisted vines,
foliage lush and green.
Jungle sounds envelop all;
Bataan's tranquil scene.
Brave men's final march.

Rolling hills with farmland plots
where food crops are grown,
not a normal battleground
near the town Bastogne.
"Nuts" to giving up.

Rocky crags peer through the drifts,
winds with biting chill.
White and black and shaded grays;
hues at Pork Chop Hill.
Peace talks stalled, they froze.

Graceful ferns sway with the breeze,
monsoon rains anon.
Multi-colored plants abound;
beauty at Khe Sanh.
Brothers died alone.

Edward W. Lull

Freedom's price—a heavy toll;
life is ours to spend.
*Dying for one's country is
dying for a friend.*
Lest we forget!

King of Equality

His legacy was Georgia-born,
and preaching was his call.
His message was a simple one:
equality for all.

At first his voice was heard by just
the faithful of his flock.
Was *equal rights for all* the key
to racial bonds unlock?

He led the marches through the South
for justice to prevail.
But often keepers of the law
put Martin King in jail.

Despite indignities he faced,
he took them all in stride
and made his plea for freedom heard;
his fame spread nationwide.

His peaceful coexistence text
became a Movement's theme.
Could races live in harmony?
That quest—his lifelong dream.

Though change proved hard for some to face
the vision he would build.
So when a bigot took his life,
his dream was unfulfilled.

Inequities and biased views
have never gone away.
But Martin Luther King's life work
continues to this day.

Edward W. Lull

Time for Change?
(A Ballade)

A politician is a tease
whose campaign takes a lofty tone,
but once elected, he'll appease
contributors who are well-known.
He acts as if his seat's a throne,
forgetting what he's there to do.
His boring speeches simply drone.
I think it's time for change, don't you?

Do you support incumbent's pleas
when he brings projects to your zone?
Are all these earmarks a disease
that voters openly condone?
They call it pork, but they are prone
to just ignore and pass them through,
then rail at how the budget's grown.
I think it's time for change, don't you?

Reform's an issue most will seize
and claim the high ground for their own,
but knowing they're their own trustees
they'll hardly starve the seeds they've sown.
So ethics bills will sink like stone
and never get atop the queue.
"Unfair!" the sponsors will bemoan.
I think it's time for change, don't you?

Is party loyalty ingrown?
Do labels form a bond like glue?
Does no one up there think alone?
I think it's time for change, don't you?

Cristoforo Colombo

Born in Genoa in 1451,
Columbus, in his teens, went to sea.
Experienced at 23, he sailed
to Khios in the Aegean.
At 25, he was bound for England,
his first time in Atlantic waters.
Off Cape St. Vincent, set upon by privateers,
Columbus' ship was burned and sank.
Clinging to floating wreckage,
he made his way to shore near Lagos.
Soon he moved on to Lisbon
to continue his seaman's life in Portugal.

For years he sailed the seas as far as Iceland and Guinea,
but the dream of reaching the riches of Marco Polo's Orient
by sailing west grew year by year.
When his proposal to King John yielded nothing,
Columbus moved to Spain.
King Ferdinand and Queen Isabella,
who yearned for trade with Asia,
accepted the Italian's plan, agreeing
to send three ships in search of routes to wealth.

On August 2, 1492, Columbus set sail from Spain
with *Niña, Pinta,* and flagship *Santa Maria.*
Educated people of the age accepted earth as a globe,
but few conceived its size. He had no fear
of falling off the earth, but he can be forgiven
when, on October 12, 1492, he sighted the Bahamas and
proclaimed that he had reached the East Indies.
What did this Italian adventurer, born Cristoforo Colombo,
sailing for Spain, really accomplish?
He was an Italian who faced the North Atlantic
in three small ships and discovered land
where Europeans had not been before—
and returned to tell his tale.

Excitement led to funding for explorers
who would follow in this burgeoning
age of exploration. Cabot, de Leon, Balboa,
Pizarro, Magellan, Cortes, de Soto all played
their roles in bringing the Americas
into the civilized world.
This Genoa-born sailor led the way.

Marty Mullendore

Autumn Observation

Vermilion
and golden leaves
are the last grudging tributes
perfidious Nature pays to her suitors.
Her encouraging words emerge on neatly pleated jonquil petals
for each spring's assembly of faithful admirers to unfold
and read back to her until the blooms grow listless at hearing them.
Then she pastes her optimism on the summer's limbs
as green and yellow missives announcing the heat
and promising the brilliance of the bluest skies.
When Sister Sunlight dims, Nature's misleading passion cools,
and she turns her head to affairs of self-indulgence.
In a show of insincere gratitude for such loyal devotion,
she decorates the autumn out of obligation.
Then she trembles slightly at the cold
and thoughtlessly shrugs off her rustling mantle.
She cares to speak no more,
yet knows that,
without fail,
the leaves
and her lovers
will find some way
to return next year.

Covenant with Death

Bind me up with silken cords,
not chains that leave their rust on me,
and still my mouth with silence sweet,
not your insane cacophony.

Imprison me in velvet robes.
Unshackle me from wooden stocks,
and close my eyes with petals' ease,
not perverse pecking of the hawks.

So bring me nectar cup to drink,
not bitter vinegar in jars,
and I will trust your baneful taste
and say, "I'm ready," to the stars.

The Blind Date

As he stood there in the dusk,
the horizontal wooden slats in our screen door
cut him into thin strips
that compelled me to reassemble him
before letting him into the house.

I didn't know what to do
with the beige Stetson he took off inside,
but I noticed the creases it had made in his hair,
and I loved the crispness of those lines
that haloed his head
and his smooth, scrubbed neck as he looked about.

Neither of us knew what to say.
Escape tried to rise in my throat,
but I swallowed it back
and followed his spotless white shirt out the door.
I became slightly soothed as I mounted
the running board of his rusty truck
and stood, for a moment, taller than he.

Nothing improved as we drove.
We were two dissonant essences
separated by the labored sound of the engine,
and miles and miles sweeping past beneath us
only widened the space
we would not cross.

After hours of humiliating apprehension,
hollow with dreariness and weary of emptiness,
we returned to the porch.
No other words and a flat, urgent kiss;
then I was again behind the safety of the slatted screen door
as it sliced his back to tatters.
I cried as he hurried away from me, wounded, into the dark.

Near Interlaken

How does the water dare to dive suicidally
From such heights
With so little plan
Of pooling place or mossy halt?

> I wish I might leap over
> The last pull of the mountain,
> Soar for an instant, all shining and golden,
> In noon-day light,
> And plummet carelessly upon rock or soft flower-heart,
> Hardly making sound.

How simple for the falcon to dip and reach
Where invisible hands first lift,
Then let him drop so calmly,
Trimming his wings and skimming along the yellow blooms!

> I wish I might spring sails
> And leap from mountain crags
> To toss upon the air.
> Like feathered kite, the coolness
> On my belly and the warmth on my back,
> I would settle into the tall grass.

How unlikely the valley blooms sprinkle
Their multi-hued faces together
So amicably, without forethought
Or design or craft!

> I wish I might lie among the flowers of man
> And smell the perfumes of lasting loves
> And feel the touch of splendid earth
> Without forethought or design or craft.

I wish to die near Interlaken,
Yes, between the lakes,
'Mid falcon, fall, dear field, and flower,
Where God may have a chance
Of finding me.

Marty Mullendore

An Investigation into the Soles of Men

The shoes of men are quite distinct,
and I believe that they are linked
to insights clear or quite obtuse
about each man, I must deduce.
His feet will tell if he's to keep
or someone out the door to sweep.

The man who wears a Sperry boat
may have a tendency to gloat
about a craft that he can sail
or one he's dreamed of while in jail.

A guy who dons a sandal sweet,
I trust, has decent-looking feet
and merely wants to cool his heels,
not have me pay for all his meals.

A loafered fellow may be fine
with character that's quite divine.
(I hope he is a business ace
and not too slack to tie a lace.)

A gentleman in polished brogue
may be aware of current vogue
and wants his feet to show some heft
but cannot tell his right from left.

I'm not so keen on western boots.
Some chaps who wear them are galoots
who like their cows more than their girls
and eat road-kill (like flattened squirrels).

The bloke who dons a sporting shoe
may not have quite enough to do,
or else he has sad feet with corns
and fallen arches that he mourns.

The gent who wears a wingtip shoe
would never wear his tie askew
and has sophisticated looks—
but spends great sums at Brothers Brooks.

Marty Mullendore

Well, science might not put much stock
in typing men by how they walk,
their footwear bold, or old, or soled,
but I tell you that I have polled.
So, women all, heed my belief
that men's shoes may lead love to grief.
Look at their feet first, I implore,
and choose those shoes you can adore!

———————— *Marty Mullendore*

A Perfect Symmetry

Although I've never had a baby,
I suspect
when a woman is enduring the final moments of labor before birth,
there are only two residents
on the island of her consciousness,
herself and her unborn child,
and they are stranded together
in an imminence of pain and freedom
that they alone can understand.
So it was with Mother and me.

However, my father and brother immediately appeared
to reassert their entitlement to her,
which they had grudgingly ceded during my arrival.
After that, I was left with only the available surplus of her.

The years passed.
When I ultimately faced the inevitability of Mother's impending death,
I sat quietly with her and held her gently,
and for the first time,
we entered into a brief period of personal revelations.

Two weeks later,
Mother was lying in a twilight of insensitivity.
Father and Brother left her room,
and it was then that she decided to die.
I lifted her hand and cupped my cheek with it,
pretending that she was the initiator
of this final intimacy.

Somewhere beyond my despair,
I was struck by the perfect symmetry
of the beginning and ending of our lives together.
Finally, Mother and I were once again
on an island with just one another—
as we had been at my birth—
intertwined once more
in an agony for one and a release for the other.

ADELE RICHARDS OBERHELMAN

The Blueridge

As we traveled down the mountain, my thoughts strayed far and wide,
from the top of "Old Grandfather" clear down the other side.

As we traveled through those mountains, in the coolness of their peaks,
we felt peace and serenity that each so fiercely seeks.

The laurel in profusion shared blossoms with the breeze;
susans in the meadows were rippling, fragrant seas.

The sky was shot with angel fluff against the brilliant blue,
a backdrop for lush foliage of every greenish hue.

The spirits of the mountain folk who labored, toiled and tilled
still whisper through the valleys, their labors at last stilled.

The heritage they left there in farm and field and glade
is rich beyond description of the sacrifices made.

Bobcats roam these mountains still, and bear and deer as well.
An eagle watches from on high, a lofty sentinel.

A cardinal in a scarlet cloak trills a freedom song,
while chipmunks scurry through the woods from warrens dark and long.

Nature shares her wonders there with anyone who seeks
to feel the ancient mysteries within her treasured peaks.

My Unsung Hero

There are no buildings named for you or plaques upon a wall,
although I know you were among the bravest of them all.
A soldier in a battle whose outcome you could not know,
who fought a skirmish every day, a melee of chemo,
of overcrowded waiting rooms and greatly harried staff
that tried to serve a patient load that should have been but half.

Each day you faced a challenge to the unformed battle plan
to foil the evil enemy in some way, small or grand.
When the knife that cuts the flesh away is finished,
it must leave both heart and brave soul undiminished,
still strong enough to offer hope to comrades in the fight
who lie in pain and sadness, wond'ring through the night:

> "Perhaps there is a treatment that has not been tried before
> or a pill to ease the suffering and pain I can't ignore."

"Ya play the hand that's dealt ya" are the words you spoke to me;
then you played that hand with bravery and quiet dignity.
There must have been a rage inside at things you knew you'd miss:
a life cut short by fate's cruel whim, you waited for death's kiss.
You never asked for pity and you never asked me why;
instead you nobly shielded me until the day you'd die.

So now I've seen a hero's face, the face of bravery,
a guy who played his whole hand out and who stayed strong for me.
Although there were no accolades—no inscriptions on a spire,
the way that you and others fought can only raise us higher.
That same brave face of kindness and courage I could see,
of quiet strength and valor I'll love eternally.

Adele Richards Oberhelman

A Promise in Pink

Resplendent pink impatiens bloom each year,
although I can't recall who put them here.
But brilliant crimson, rose and scarlet grow
from softest Princess Pink, almost aglow,
to hottest fuchsia—petals blush and preen.
Their seeds flung far and wide, from pistils green
produced these flaming beauties that I see.
Then suddenly—a flash of memory,
reminding me *you* sowed the first few seeds
that now proliferate among the weeds
and shout their clever message of survival . . . .
With spring will come each blossom's pink revival.
A promise in these lavish blooms, I think,
that life goes on in vibrant shades of pink.

—Adele Richards Oberhelman

Aurora Borealis

My dad woke me up in the middle of the night
to observe a rare and spectacular sight.
He took me outside in the dark, yet bright,
to see a shimmering rainbow of light.

Lights of all colors danced across the sky,
so vibrant I could almost hear them cry.
They swirled in bright, undulating light,
pulsing waves, exploding with solar might.

An experience he wanted to share with me,
this sight that many never get to see.
I wish I could tell him how precious to me
is that brilliant and special memory.

I Spring Eternal

When Pandora opened the forbidden box,
she permitted escape of assorted "pox."
Fear and Anger came rushing out;
Grief and Despair were quickly about.
The world soon filled with assorted ills,
against which humans possessed few skills.

But *I* was hidden in my special place,
an eternal friend to the human race.
I've heard petitions from folks under stress.
I offer comfort to those in distress.
Whether grieving lost love or burdened with shame,
the gift *I* give is always the same.

You will know what it is when you hear my name:

    HOPE.

—*Adele Richards Oberhelman*

Celebrating Technology,
or
What Are We All Smiling About?

Technology would make work more effective
and give us all more time to just relax.
Instead of mail by way of postal service,
we'd get it there much faster via fax.

Computers store all necessary info,
so no longer is there any need to file.
Fingernails stay nice a whole lot longer,
resulting in the clerk's delighted smile.

Technology seemed like a panacea
with everything we'd need to know online,
'til it became a "wolf inside sheep's clothing,"
devourer of relationships and time.

Earbuds and iPads and downloads made inroads
and Kindles leave book pages dusty.
There are prisoners now to a virtual life,
who consider the internet trusty.

Their pseudo-friends send voice mail and text,
and Facebook shares every detail
of their own daily lives and that of their pets,
as their real-life relationships fail.

BUT

The Hubble has shown us an Ultra Deep Field
of vast galaxies quite beguiling.
Since our place in the heavens is really quite small,
perhaps Someone is watching us,

. . . *smiling.*

Linda Partee

Just Like Me

My quilt lies aging and worn,
each scrap has a story to tell;
from hardscrabble roots into being,
made rich by its creator's hands.
    Just like me.

Plain beginnings, but unique
like fingerprints, none are the same.
Perhaps out of vogue, though still valued,
the sum of its parts holds the charm.
    Just like me.

Durable, adaptable,
cozy and always practical—
the finished work earns status and praise
while the knots are hidden inside.
    Just like me.

Aprons, gowns and pinafores—
simple remnants of yesterday;
every piece cradling an old soul
in a sentimental new skin.
    Just like me.

Fabric pieces of lifetimes
held close together by a thread;
fraying heartaches around the edges,
stronger stitching holding the core.
    Just like me.

Caretaker of memories—
fragments embedded in the heart;
touching and connecting with others
to create new beauty and life.
    Just like me.

Pomp & Circumstances

The air undulates with heat and the long day begins,
as it always does, on this day of expectations.
Come together for its unfolding and sing its spirited songs.
Listen to the snapping of breeze-caught cloth, as you remember why.

Make ready to feel the steady drumming thunder,
to hear the fluting gathering calls of pipes,
their cadence marking the coming of corps and banners
marching in waves of brotherly configurations.

Picnics spread, feeding visions of our forefathers
drunk from sipping at the well of courage.
Drowsy babes and restless children on blanketed grass wait;
window-framed faces and chairs on cracked porches anticipate.

Furtive eyes search the sky for the dusky curtain to descend,
while arms link and hands clasp on this eve of celebration.
Reunion, the symbol of old war reflections, sighs with promise,
as chins lift toward the darkening of the night.

Like cannon's shot, the birth of freedom repeats its cry,
unleashed in a fiery brilliance of dreams.
Reminders of a long-ago pledge, not of entitlement or arrogance—
each spark a patriot living on through a cacophony by design.

The air is filled with ash-fall when the long day finally yawns,
as it always does, following this ritual of renewal.
Once complacent hearts carry freedom's beat,
drafting the vows of future guardians to its cause.

Homemade Preserves

High up in the cupboard, a jelly-jar
glass floating Dad's invisible image,
still stuck with a faded *"Preserves"* label,
reflects our homemade nurture and values.

Self-taught carpenter of words and actions,
he built a solid foursquare pedestal
for his two daughters to stand tall upon,
much like preserves settle firm on a shelf.

Few homespun homilies left his hushed lips,
but living life with wisdom's recipes
for honesty, integrity, duty,
respect, truth and blue-ribbon character,
he spread his jar of preserved principles
for us, anchoring our feet forever.

Knowing the jeweled fruit held all the sweetness
of life's promise, we took ample spoonfuls
and never wished jars empty of credo
hand-me-downs, like being true to your word,
standing up for your beliefs and country,
or being faithful to loved ones and friends.

Unlike glass, his mettle unbreakable—
stronger than easy fast-food excuses,
Daddy never deemed truth too expensive.
These old-fashioned home-gelled virtues preserved,
gave of their essence to ensure the same,
so there'd be no doubt what you'd find inside.

Linda Partee

Just the Tip of the Iceberg
(A Sonnet)

It's *Crest* then *Glide* and *Scope* to start my day;
Caress and *Herbal Essence* scrubs me clean.
Then *Secret* keeps the odors all at bay,
and powder dusts its opalescent sheen.

My face is daubed in retinol's white cream;
applied to hair for volume—blue *Lagoom*.
Clinique will mask the spots, restoring gleam,
conceal the bags, then blush the cheeks for bloom.

Fill meager brows and blink with *Fabulash*,
draw lips with *Revlon's* shade of "Copperglow;"
then body-butter limbs before I dash—
Escada spritz, and finally, dryer's blow.

Routines of women reek commercial bunk,
cuz heaven knows that God don't make no junk.

Wavelength

Insignificant, as one speck of sand
   windblown to the edge of a dampened shore,
I watch the blustery twilight darken,
   life's shadows growing large about me—looming.
Ocean's rhythmic turbulence curiously calming,
   mystifying, hypnotizing, mesmerizing;
an invitation from the source of Revelation,
   of Genesis and Armageddon,
to Forever and Eternity.

Daylight's end transfigures nature's playground
to an altar of reflection and prayer;
   heartstrings loosed and humbled—opening, spilling
tithes of tears, gratitude and wonder—
   sucking ebb, swallowing up heart secrets.
The gift of peace rides in on foam-frothed waves
   to fulfill this rite of spiritual cleansing;
hugging drawn knees, I wait enraptured
   for my soul to be washed by the sea.

Linda Partee

So Hearts Will Sing
(A Triolet)

To write the songs that hearts will sing,
rejoice or weep and understand,
use thought-filled words, subdue the sting,
to write the songs that hearts will sing.
Life's common feelings know the ring
when truth and love work hand-in-hand
to write the songs that hearts will sing,
rejoice or weep and understand.

Mark Reardon

Sacred Ground

Many centuries ago a forest stood here.
Its trees gave life to those who wandered near.
As they traveled through the woods,
The Wind whispered lightly through the trees,
"Tread gently here, my friends, for this is sacred ground."

The farmer came and cleared the arbors.
His wheat gave people life and ardor.
As he sweat behind his plow,
The Wind whispered lightly with a breeze,
"Tread gently here, my friends, for this is sacred ground."

One day two Armies arrived
And set up camps on either side.
As they prepared for things that soldiers fear,
The Wind whispered lightly in their ears,
"Tread gently here, my friends, for this is sacred ground."

Both Armies awoke that day
And felt the Sun and its rays.
Then the cannons exploded with noise so great,
No one could hear the Wind decree,
"Tread gently here, my friends, for this is sacred ground."

Then at once the cannons ceased.
In the silence, thousands lined up dress-right dressed,
And thousands on the other side shoulder-to-shoulder pressed.
No one listened as the Wind once more uttered,
"Tread gently here, my friends, for this is sacred ground."

The Sun beat down and on they marched,
Not a breath of air to fill their lungs so parched.
As they tramped across the field,
The Wind gave one last plea,
"Tread gently here, my friends, for this is sacred ground."

Once again the cannons roared,
Cutting men down as wheat before the scythe.
As forward they drove, over the fence, across the road,
The Wind to itself could only sigh,
"Tread gently here, my friends, for this is sacred ground."

In the end, men on either side stared in shock at what they'd done.
As they huddled close and sucked for air,
The Wind rose gently and drifted by.
It had no need to whisper,
"Tread gently here, my friends, for this is sacred ground."

When evening came,
The living looked across the field and cried in pain.
As they watched humanity seep into the soil,
The Wind returned and brought the Rain.
Together they washed the field and memories made this Sacred Ground.

One hundred fifty years have passed.
People rush across the field so fast.
And as they stare at rows of Unknowns' graves,
Can they hear the Wind whisper still,
"Tread gently here, my friends, for this is sacred ground"?

Many centuries hence a forest will stand here.
Its trees will give life to those who wander near.
As strangers dig among the graves to find out what happened here,
Will someone finally heed the Wind as it whispers lightly through the trees,
"Tread gently here, my friends, for this is sacred ground"?

The Pleasure of the Mountain

A bright red orb sits precariously upon its peak.
The snow-white crests call to me
And its three undulating mounds slope down
As if inviting me to immerse myself in its beauty.
Narrow, brownish rivulets wend their way down its sides
Wetting the fertile bowl below
And feeding fruit awaiting at its base.
I stare in wonder as small, tannish rocks
Slide through the snow to let me know it's melting.

I wish my power of will were somewhat stronger,
But this banana split can't last very much longer.

Lake George Morn

The lake is a pane of blue-tinted glass.
Not a ripple disturbs its glacial perfection.
The Sun shines brightly in the azure sky.
Its rays bounce off the beautiful glass
Reflecting like diamonds belonging to God.

The Emerald Mountains stand guard
Protecting Heaven's perfect scene.
Unaware of the beauty of their many greens,
They silently stand their eternal watch,
Reflecting with the diamonds in the glass.

The water laps gently at the shore
With its quiet symphony played so often before.
Its music soothes and lightens the soul.
No other sound disturbs this morn
But the songs of birds greeting the dawn.

How Do We Begin to Heal?

April Eighteenth of Sixty-Five, the terrible war has come to an end.
The smoke of Richmond's smoldering ruins
Choked the breath from the city's soul.
And the stench of fear, bitterness and hatred
Brought untold tears that made it impossible to speak.
In their hearts the people cried,
"How do we begin to heal?"

Amidst the joy and noise of victory,
In Washington a single shot went almost unheard.
The bullet choked the breath from the nation's soul.
And the stench of fear, bitterness, and hatred
Brought untold tears that made it impossible to speak.
In their hearts the people cried,
"How do we begin to heal?"

At St. Paul's the people gathered to ask for guidance.
The service should have given comfort and solace to those in the pews.
At least here, they thought, life could seem normal.
Yet even in God's house there was no relief
From the transformed world the war had wrought.
In their hearts the people cried,
"How do we begin to heal?"

At Communion, as they prayed for God to bring them answers,
A lone black man stepped forward, walked to the rail, and knelt.
The minister halted and seemed too dazed to move.
The congregation froze and gasped as one.
There in silent horror,
In their hearts the people cried,
"How do we begin to heal?"

Then a tall, white-haired man, aged beyond his years,
Stood, walked to the rail, and knelt beside the man of color.
Together they received the Lord.
Still suffering from the agonizing pains of war and defeat,
Robert E. Lee would lead the way
And show the country
How to begin to heal.

———————————————————————— Mark Reardon

Christmas Mittens

Each and every night throughout the year,
With balls of yarn in bags about her feet,
She sat serenely rocking in her sphere
Knitting mittens till they were all complete.

The needles sang with steady click-clicking,
When they were released from their darkened dens.
And her fingers played at fiddle sticking,
While the yarn turned into Christmas mittens.

Soft and warm and waiting for the first snow,
They filled the stockings on each Christmas Eve.
Each stitch was smoothly knitted in its row
As if a Christmas angel did the weave.

Each year I think of what those mittens meant:
Our Mother's love was most magnificent.

The Color Had All Been Taken Away

The color had all been taken away.
The first day was so bold and bright.
All that remains are shades of gray.

To the moon he promised we'd go someday.
Without him, though, it no longer seemed right.
The color had all been taken away.

We had no doubt he could lead the way.
But he flashed though our lives like a meteorite.
All that remains are shades of gray.

It was all perverted on that November day.
We could only watch in tearful fright.
The color had all been taken away.

We watched the scenes in complete dismay.
How could they have put out such a light?
All that remains are shades of gray.

The last day was so cold, and we had no words to say
As we cried goodbye to our youthful knight.
The color had all been taken away.
All that remains are shades of gray.

Mark Reardon

Terry Shepard

Elegy for Ricky

I could not write this

when you left us on your journey home.
It hurt too much to ever say goodbye,
son, nephew, friend, you were to us.
You taught us love, your pure giving way.

You were the listener, always by our sides,
who looked at us with joy in your face.
You reflected the best in all of us
and made us feel our strengths were recognized.

The funeral parlor, packed by those you touched,
overflowed to porch and parking lot.
They spoke of you in glowing, lively phrase,
appreciative of all your generous ways.

A legacy of love you left behind.
A gift of simple presence you bestowed.
The family ties you knitted still are strong,
dear baby, boy, and man who journeyed home.

My Poet Path

I write because
it's the only sane thing to do,
with all the thoughts inside my head.
I tweak these thoughts to clear a path,
like a gardener weeding a flower bed
that leaves behind only what
she wants to grow.

As poet, I am
a gardener of words,
their meaning a palette
of humble treasure
that leads me to
something deeper,
surprising,
bigger.

Where
few words,
choice words,
connect

me
to my
soul.

Terry Shepard

Mid-September

Black shadows fly across a cloudless sky
as their cacophony of greetings fill the scene.
Beneath their wings, locusts hum loud sonatas
from blades of grass hunched over
with ripened seeds.

Inside a dense gardenia laced with creamy stars
hops a homeless wren from stem to stem.
She chirps her mid-September salutation
and lone goodbye to summer's
nesting season.

My Little Town

This little town has grown so large
from mooring creek to battle yard.
I can still remember when
the first strip mall intruded in.

The subtle change to unkempt space,
concrete poured on plowing fields,
fallen trees and smoke-filled skies—
I wish I could have stopped the change,

retained the peace, the call of birds,
or even the sound of a hunter's gun,
a cow's moo, a farmer's call.
Change is all I've ever known.

This is still my little town
stretched out wide as a modern quilt.
I reach my hand into the soil
between the man-made patches.

It feels as though it's just been plowed
but not for wheat or barley field.
Landscaped yards fill up the space;
useful things are plucked away.

Gardeners turn a snobbish face,
forget the ones who knew the land,
as if there were no honored past,
as if my town did not exist.

Terry Shepard

Mother Oak

Sweeping breezes wander past her mooring;
Seeping cold reaches 'neath her bark,
her changing leaves flow with autumn colors.
Red and gold, they hug her, then depart.

Wayward waltzing in the frosted woodland,
shifting gently with the spinning wind,
twirling, swirling, whirling, they go dancing,
settling contentedly in the end.

Thick and piled in heaps on forest lowland,
sleeping past their gold to dusty brown,
they warm the dampened earth for baby acorns
who suckle filtered water seeping down.

Groundhog Day

"It is illegal to be a vagrant,"
stated a homeless man in
Richmond, Virginia.

Beneath the snow
the daffodils spring buds,
while roots of calla lilies twine
with hidden plants weaving secret webs.
They hold the dampened earth in such a way
that life within the winter garden stays.

Somewhere shaded berries hang
to feed the birds that stay in residence.
In forks of oaks, squirrels arrange their leaves
to stop the drips snow is sending down,
while footprints stroll
through laden branches bowed.

Are they prints from groundhog feet,
his forecast told?
I missed his graying chubby face.
Against the sky, leafless myrtles climb
with bark as smoothed as sacred polished stone.
They edge the asphalt road
that wanders past the place where nature goes.

Does it matter what the groundhog said
to those dependent on the weather for a meal?
I ponder in my heated living space
so far removed from struggle that's in view.
I will never know that glory of survival,
worship of the stars and the moon,
pray for rising of the sun
to warm me once the night is gone.

Terry Shepard

Edith Piedmont Stoke

Enough Sense to Go Out in the Rain

No one jogs, walks the dog, or strolls
coffee-in-hand among dewy flowers.
Walking alone, I feel strangely untethered,
ease into the surrounding rhythms.
Everything green drips and bends slightly
in deference to life-giving rain.

The breeze sprays a gray, slanting drip
from socked-in skies. Splats feel like puppy dog licks
on leathery skin and tickle cleanly on my tongue.
Four rabbits scamper unhurriedly between grass and woods.
Birdsongs are infrequent, lacking volume and insistence.
Brightly colored feathers are hidden from morning.

A leafy area is unusually soft and silent underfoot.
Across water-skimmed pavement worms scribble
cursive mysteries. One—plump, wriggling, pale-pink
as my own sun-shy belly—evokes a smile of unexpected kinship.
How soothing the solitary "slap, slap" of alternating feet
carrying me forward on the path, all senses awakened.

The sound chants me back to before television,
before Doppler, before air-conditioning,
when a summer storm meant relief
from unrelenting heat and drought;
back to a time when Mother
laid down her fan, tossed aside her sandals, and rushed
barefoot onto the grass, as we children ran into the street
wet-headed and shirtless,
squealing and splashing in every puddle.

Essence

> *We have a soul at times.*
> *No one's got it non-stop . . . .*
>
> Wisława Szymborska

Ah, but you did not know my father.
His gift was the way he embraced
this unfolding surprise called life
with gratitude, a bit of humor,
and unbounded passion.

He managed to fill the lives
of his twelve children
with sacred music, lively debate,
opera, fast-paced card games,
barbershop harmony, practical jokes,
Sunday drives on the Blue Ridge Parkway,
and enough "nickels to spend"
to make us think ourselves rich.

His soulful engagement of the ordinary
was most vivid while presiding
over the family ritual of table.
Without fail he bowed his head before supper,
beseeching God's blessing on those present
and absent, and on *these Thy gifts . . .*
from Thy bountiful hands.
He served the meat to Mother first;
vegetables were passed
and his litany began.
Keep your napkin in your lap.
Chew with your mouth closed.
Eat over your plate.
Let someone else talk.
Then, in an amazing breach of etiquette,

Who wants some essence?

With a mischievous twinkle he would
break bread into small pieces
and sop the seasoned juices from the platter,
making sure each child got a share of the goodness
dripping from his hand.

Edith Piedmont Stoke

Contrails

for Stephen

It is one of those diamond-bright days when
colorless cold polishes bark to platinum,
bermuda to gold, sky to sapphire. Crisp,
hard-edged, a good day to contemplate
solid ground underfoot
and steamy breath before me.
Crunch, breathe, crunch, breathe,
solitary plodding
until a jet bellows up from the south
spuming a throaty, white cut across the blue.
The winding trail arches north
for a long time as the tightrope vapor
frays soft at the edges,
feathers to snowy egret plumes,
then finally spins out
cotton candy for a feasting god.
Crunch, breathe, crunch, breathe,
behind me trail morphing whispers,
another path across the earth.

Another Visit

for Jeff and Dan

The image from an earlier time
stills me into reverie. Two anonymous brothers,
blonde mops, bare feet, perched on river-wall steps,
staring down at a taut string dropped into the water.
Both dirty enough to be having fun, clean enough to
appear idyllic in cut-off jeans and white sailor tops.

The sons of forty years ago leap in my heart . . .
my boys, separated by two years, yet inseparable
in their carefree pursuit of good times and adventure.
I want to tousle their sweaty hair, clasp their grimy hands,
go inside for peanut butter sandwiches
with iced lemonade. I want to look again into
those wide blue eyes, loving, questioning, believing
that good guys always win and every dream
can have a happy ending.

Now successful men, with children of their own,
both have pulled up many prizes . . .
and surprises . . . from unsure waters. All loves
are not pure. Some questions
a mother can never answer. Wounds
aren't so neatly washed, kissed,
and covered with a Superman band-aid;
some leave scars. And the eyes,
oh, those big blue eyes have seen more
than any mother wants her sons to see.

With gratitude to the artist, I slip the old greeting card
back into my desk drawer where it will rest until
I want to hold my children again. Then the image
will waken those beautiful boys who play
and have life deep in my heart
until my last breath is drawn.

———————————————————— *Edith Piedmont Stoke*

The Motherline Is a Circle

for Angela and Rosemarie

Subtle but sacred,
the instinctive lift and curve
of a grandmother's arms to cradle
what a daughter hands forward.
The infant girl meets my gaze
with eyes like pools of night
bringing light from ancient stars.
Her mouth, a pink, milk-laced yawn
closes softly and pulls,
savoring the aftertaste of mother.
She snuffles and burrows
into relaxed, milkless breasts, seeking
a soft dry place to rest her head.
One tiny ear presses against my heart
where the ancestral grandmothers wait
to sing their lullaby. My lips find
the soft diamond of her crown
pulsing with a fragrance, an ecstasy,
perhaps some memory of origin and angels,
or the mingled perfumes
of a strong line of women.

Hearthcall

Something rises in me
with the Harvest Moon,
waxes with rusting dogwoods.
Orange pumpkin orbs
beam an autumnal pull
toward ritual cooking.

I want to fill every pot, bowl, and jar
with earthy comfort foods:
fresh tomato sauce, spicy chili,
steaming chicken and dumplings,
pork and beans from scratch,
minestrone with tag-ends of summer,
applesauce from the first autumn crop,
and of course, pesto, pesto, pesto,
so not one leaf of basil
remains for the frost.

We can't possibly eat it all!
It's as if ancient crones whisper
their woman-chant in the chill,
*Come into our circle, feed the fire
with your life . . . reap, cook, hasten
to pay forward all that is bountiful.*

Peter Trainor

Dawn:
Nuevo Vallarta, Mexico

Morning,
as yet unborn
behind the mountains,
dark-shadowed attendants
expectantly standing
in pre-dawn darkness.

My balcony seat, a
perfect observation deck
for the Phoenix
of reawakening transformation
channeled by the new daylight.
I, a silent witness,
transfixed
as morning's tentacles
creep through the cloud cover.

From black to blue
to variegated shades of green,
the mountains grin back at me
in celebration of new life.
They are the base of an
expanding golden throne.
My eyes drop
to the river playing at their feet,
now bathed in the flow of gold
merging its sparkle
into a birthday ribbon
of blue-green refreshment from the heat
already rising in praise
of a borning light.

The sleeping egrets at water's
edge come to life
with the call of nature's clock.
We break fast together.
The river shimmers,
clouds melt,
the sky blues brilliantly.

Reborn.
As I applaud their effort,
in a barely audible breath
the mountains sigh in resignation.
My enjoyment of this creation,
their already deconstructing déjà vu.

Maine

The green Adirondacks
sit empty on the dock, filled only
with the wet breeze
that drifts across Great Pond.
I stand among the pines
awaiting that familiar cry
that defines a Maine lake. But
it's too late. The season
has passed, and loon-less, the lake
wavers in the misty
late-September rain.

A forest of memories
enfolds me. The empty cottage
still pulses with your past presence
in faint echo—your unpacking
from everyday
to holiday. I imagine
the reverse process—expression
of regret at "times up" forced departure.

The sighs of the pines
mock my own, as irregular
sputter of rain-tears
caress the forest floor.
I look back at the dock.
The green Adirondacks
sit empty, alone. Silent
sentinels of a summer's end,
yet deafening in their invitation
of open arms stretched
in anticipation of your
seasonal tomorrows.
I smile at their backs
and turn away.

Womb of Life

The sea. Womb of life.
Full of life still.

I float. A voyeur
sneaking a peek into the fluids
my primal ancestors crawled
from. I can no longer live
there. Expelled, banished,

but so anxious to reconnect
with the undulating majesty
as I breathe through a tube. Artificial
webbing encases my feet, stabilizers
in the no-longer-familiar currents

as I watch the unobstructed clarity
of magical colors. Effortless beauty in the ebb
and flow, oblivious to the turmoil above. Though
indiscriminately disturbed every chance we get.

Through my fogging, sea-encroaching lenses,
a pang of sudden sadness
constricts my chest as I wish,
sometimes,
I could go home again.

Peter Trainor

The Entertainer

She sings jazz.
Thirty-eight, looks younger,
sings older. We listen with ears
and eyes. Soaking it in as she
perches on a stool
using the mike
like an instrument,
a trombone, back
and forth to accent
the tune, inflect a lyric.

The keyboardist on the same
page. Following each other
like dancers exchanging
the lead. Her fingers,
long and thin, tap the seat
rhythmically imitating
the progression of each number.
Beautiful voice. Uniquely unblemished.
Complements her look. Marketable combination.
A thought: so what are you doing
in a Mexican resort wine bar?

Set over, I ask.
They are in the process
of "putting something together."
She hands me a card. Email, website.
"Look for us on iTunes."
We thank them,
leave a tip,
and go to dinner.
The card, forgotten
in the flow of conversation,
is left on the table.

The Ending

A slice of life
flows through my veins.
Pick up your pieces
and board your plane.

Back door slams,
head lifts from arms.
Where in our past
was there any harm?

Down my back roads
we joined together
while I held your face
in hurricane weather.

Goodbyes were lost
in a storm's confusion.
Our pain commingles—
an intimate transfusion.

So long. Farewell.
You've got to go.
I say, "It's too late,"
but you already know.

9/11/11

Ten years gone,
with no less pain,
but with hate that grows as steady
as the new construction
filling the void
of Ground Zero.

We roam, zombie-like,
amid the ruins
of lost lessons harboring
the unity of justice and peace.
Surviving in the contradiction
of a fading world sympathy
while drowning in our inability
to actually touch each other.
Insulated by our personal silos
of unholy ground.

Second chances
still lie in ruins behind the façade
of crumbled walls,
rebuilt to new majestic heights,
simply blinding us to life's currents
which eventually dump us
all in the same sea.

Tears of blood
swept up in the debris
now contaminate the landfill
of unmet expectations.
In the anguish of unfulfilled dreams,
the shadows close in to smother
all hope of forgiveness.

Reconciliation
eludes our desperate grasp
like the rushing ash cloud
of collapsed promises
ghosting through our hungry fingers,
still evolving from our dedication
to desolation.
Ten years gone.

Contributors

James City Poets

Joan Ellen Casey

Joan Casey has made a career of writing and editing educational materials, beginning at Dodd, Mead Publishers in New York and honing her skills at several reputable houses. Among her accomplishments are: a Science and Math high-school curriculum for the U.S. Office of Economic Opportunity, a teachers' and students' guide to Colonial Williamsburg, and a qualitative study of how adults "make meaning" of their educational experiences, which earned her a doctorate from the College of William & Mary in 1998. But Joan's real passion is for her poetry. Although never seeking publication, she entered her first contest in 2011 and won the Metrorail Public Art Project Award from the Poetry Society of Virginia. With the eye of a photographer and the palette of an avid reader, Joan here writes about traveling to South America.

Gillian Dawson

Gillian Dawson grew up and received her education in England, obtaining a Master's degree in French and Spanish. She lived in Australia for five years, then came to America in 1965. She and her husband and children lived in various places in this country, coming to Virginia in 1975. They first lived in Newport News, then moved to Williamsburg in 1985. It was not until the 1980's that Gillian started writing mostly humorous poetry for the enjoyment of her colleagues in the break rooms at Colonial Williamsburg. There she worked as a historical interpreter for fourteen years, moving to the Museums in 1988 as a monitor. She began attending the Williamsburg Saturday morning readings, joined the Sunday afternoon poetry workshop, and finally took the Christopher Wren Association beginner and intermediate poetry-writing classes.

Edward W. Lull

In his first career, Ed Lull served in the U.S. Navy, primarily in submarines. He later served as president and chairman of The Professional Group of Fairfax. In 1998, he began his writing career and joined the Poetry Society of Virginia (PSV); he served four terms as President and is a Life Member. His publications include: *Cabin Boy to Captain: A Sea Story; Where Giants Walked; The Sailors: Birth of a Navy;* and *Bits and Pieces: A Memoir.* For ten years, Ed hosted a three-day poetry festival for PSV and has organized monthly poetry readings in Williamsburg since 2001. He is chairman of the Emerson Society of Williamsburg and a member of the Christopher Newport University Writers Council. Ed earned his B.S. at the U.S. Naval Academy and M.S. at George Washington University.

Marty Mullendore

Born and raised in Texas, Marty Mullendore embarked upon what would be a thirty-year-long adventure as a military wife, replete with considerable travel and a multitude of addresses. She found living in Heidelberg, Germany, for ten years to be her most significant experience. Over the course of some forty-five years, Marty taught English language and literature and also worked in both the private sector and the federal government as a human resources specialist and manager. Having moved to Williamsburg in 1995, she retired from teaching in 2010. Her B.A. is in English, and her M.A. is in Human Resources Management.

Adele Richards Oberhelman

Adele Oberhelman, a Pennsylvania native and retired Executive Secretary/Administrator, worked for the Aluminum Company of America in Pittsburgh; the U.S. Army Aviation Materiel Laboratories at Fort Eustis, Virginia; and Anheuser-Busch Company in Williamsburg. Over the years, Adele has written poetry from time to time, but not in any concentrated way until she joined the James City Poets. A resident of Williamsburg, she has one son, a physicist and systems engineer, who lives with his wife in Fairfax, Virginia.

Linda Partee

Linda Partee creates much memoir-based poetry, written in both traditional format and free-verse styles, enjoying the challenges each type presents. A native Californian, she claims to have teethed on Robert Louis Stevenson's *A Child's Garden of Verses* and treasures her silk-bound 1898 edition. Linda earned a B.A. in Communications and M.A. in Speech Pathology from California State University, Fullerton. She has recently been inspired to expand from technical writing into prose, essay, and poetry. During a 28-year career as an educator and administrator, she authored several educational books and teacher resources and in 2005 wrote *Apron Strings,* a family cookbook. Mother of two, grandmother of five, Linda is a member of the Poetry Society of Virginia.

Mark Reardon

Mark Reardon was born and raised in the beautiful Adirondack Mountains of New York. He had the honor to serve in the U.S. Army for forty-four years as soldier and civilian. Mark began his writing career in a beginning poetry-writing workshop with the Christopher Wren Association at the College of William & Mary and has continued to develop his skills in local workshops. A member of the Poetry Society of Virginia, he is retired and lives in Williamsburg with his wife Cindi.

Terry Shepard

Terry Shepard has been a resident of Williamsburg since 1984. She was born in Verdun, France, to a military father stationed there and grew up in Newport News. She received a baccalaureate degree in commercial art from Virginia Commonwealth University. After graduation Terry worked for NASA Langley Research Center, first as a technical and scientific photographer, then as a director, writer, and producer of documentaries. She currently enjoys writing poetry, spending time with her grandson, and gardening.

Williamsburg Poetry Workshop

Flora Bolling Adams

A native Virginian born in the mountain village of Flat Gap in Wise County, Flora Adams attended Radford State Teachers College (now Radford University) for two years before transferring to the University of Maryland and receiving a B.S. degree. She thought she was the only girl in the world who had to wait tables to stay in school. Later she earned a Master's degree in Education while working at the elementary-school level. Flora writes stories and poems for children and for others who choose to stay young. She finds herself toying with the child's mind in the adult and believes that every piece of literature holds a special message waiting for appropriate delivery. For the past three years she has served as President of the Williamsburg Poetry Guild. After her husband Kelsey passed, Flora moved from Williamsburg to Toano, where she and son Kirk listen to the same music and welcome the three others, who bring her seven grandchildren and three greats for her to adore and listen to their rhymes.

Angela Anselmo

Born and raised in New York City, Angela Anselmo lived there and on Long Island for most of her life. She earned a B.S. degree from Columbia University and a Master's degree in Community Health from Long Island University. Angela practiced and taught nursing at several hospitals and schools, including the State University of New York at Stony Brook and at Farmingdale. While living on Long Island, she joined a local writers' group called Taproot and began writing prose. With encouragement from the leader and other members, she turned to poetry. The challenge of expressing feelings and images in precise ways appealed to her. Angela draws inspiration from ordinary, everyday events and sometimes from the unusual, humorous aspects of life. After retirement, she and her husband Joe moved to Williamsburg in 1999. She has been volunteering at Colonial Williamsburg for thirteen years, is co-founder of the Williamsburg Poetry Workshop, a member of the Poetry Society of Virginia, and has published two books of poetry and a poetry calendar.

Norma Beuschel

Norma Beuschel was born in Brooklyn and lived in that area for the first twenty-nine years of her life. She was a member of the third class to graduate from Queens College, City University of New York. After graduation, she worked as a translator and interpreter for the Federal Bureau of Investigation and censored mail in French, Spanish, and Portuguese for the U.S. Post Office. In 1951 she and her husband began working overseas—first in Turkey, then on Guam, and in Iran, France, and Germany. In each place she taught high school language classes. Returning to the United States in 1973, Norma taught French, Spanish, and German at Neptune High School in New Jersey until her retirement in 1997. A few years later, she moved to Williamsburg because her younger son, a Department of Defense employee, had been transferred to nearby Fort Eustis. As an atheist, a liberal, and a supporter of abortion and gay rights, she says she feels uncomfortable in the politically and culturally conservative Williamsburg area.

Ann Marie Boyden

Having started out to be an actress, Ann Marie Boyden also toyed with the idea of playing golf for a living—all the while writing poems. The most logical compromise seemed to be advertising. After working in television, radio, and advertising, Ann Marie started et al, inc, a full service advertising agency. The agency was sold and she moved to Washington, D.C., to become Executive Director of the American Institute of Architects Trust. She retired to Williamsburg to write poems and prose, play golf, take and print pictures, and cook.

Thayer Cory

Thayer Cory was raised with four siblings in New Jersey but feels most at home on the shore of eastern Long Island and in the wilds of New England. After college (political science) and graduate school (psychology and religion) in the Boston area, she moved to Williamsburg where she raised two children and helped raise two stepchildren. She and her husband, Tom Weet, are avid hikers and have walked parts of the Camino de Santiago in France and Spain. Thayer's work as a psychotherapist in both public and private settings for thirty-five years continually inspires her to see the world from many perspectives, and her involvement in Williamsburg Friends Meeting keeps her grounded in a spiritual community. Both experiences nurture and inform her poetry. Her poems search for the threads that keep us connected to human relationships, to the natural world and to the divine.

Ron Landa

A Chicago-area native, Ron Landa attended several universities, eventually earning a Ph.D. in American diplomatic history from Georgetown University in 1970. He briefly taught at College Misericordia and George Washington University. For thirty-nine years he served as a historian for the U.S. Department of State and for the Office of the Secretary of Defense, where he edited volumes in the documentary series, *Foreign Relations of the United States*, and co-authored *The McNamara Ascendancy, 1961-1965*. Ron began writing poetry in 2002. His collection of poems, *Drops in a Bucket*, was published in 2011. He enjoys ballroom and line dancing, golf, lawn bowling, travel, studying foreign languages, reading old-time mystery writers like Agatha Christie and Eric Ambler, and rooting for the Chicago Cubs. Ron and his wife Barb have three children and three grandchildren.

Don Loop

Don Loop grew up in Blacksburg, Virginia. Upon graduation from Blacksburg High School, he joined the U.S. Navy at age 17 and became a member of the Submarine Service. During his time with the Navy, he obtained a private pilot's license, after which he attended Lynchburg College in Virginia for one year and St. John's College in Annapolis, Maryland, for another year. Having spent much time at sea, including one ocean crossing, Don sailed into Urbanna Creek, Virginia, in 2002, where he presently lives ashore. He has a son and a daughter, three grandchildren, and is now unmarried. Don earns his living as a multi-skilled craftsman.

Edith Piedmont Stoke

Edith Stoke grew up in the Shenandoah Valley of Virginia as one of twelve children. After graduating from DePaul School of Nursing, she married and began following her husband's career to Europe and many parts of the United States. Edith raised three children before taking her first poetry class at the Haden Institute in Charlotte, North Carolina, seventeen years ago. Now retired in Williamsburg, she continues to be active in the local poetry community. Many of her poems are intended to preserve the characters and stories of her lively extended family. Edith also finds that writing keeps her deeply connected to her experiences and her own evolving questions.

Peter Trainor

Born and raised in the New York/New Jersey metropolitan area, Peter Trainor has been a resident of Williamsburg since 2003. As Vice President, Sales and Marketing, for Penetron Specialty Products, he spends much of his time travelling throughout the United States and Canada. He does not recall when he started writing, but he discovered the poems of e e Cummings in junior high, which influenced his early years. Now Peter writes song lyrics, short stories, and poetry to ground him in today's hectic pace. An avid runner, he enjoys golf and the *New York Times* crossword puzzles. Peter and his wife Debbie have two daughters and six grandchildren.

CPSIA information can be obtained at www.ICGtesting.com
Printed in the USA
BVOW03s1444140813

328455BV00004B/16/P